MAKING A DIFFERENCE:

A Parent's Guide to Advocacy and Community Action

Diane J. Charnov and Carolyn Rutsch

Children's Resources International, Inc.
Washington, DC

The Soros Foundations/Open Society Institute is a network of foundations, programs, and institutions established and supported by philanthropist George Soros to foster the development of open societies around the world, particularly in the former communist countries of Central and Eastern Europe and the former Soviet Union. To this end, the Step by Step Program was developed as a collaborative project of the Open Society Institute, the network of Soros Foundations, Children's Resources International, and the International Step by Step Association and its members.

Children's Resources International, a nonprofit organization located in Washington, DC, is dedicated to improving the quality of educational experiences and opportunities for children and their families in the United States and internationally.

Children's Resources International, Inc.
5039 Connecticut Ave., NW, Suite One
Washington, DC 20008
202-363-9002 *phone*
202-363-9550 *fax*
E-mail: info@crinter.com
www.childrensresources.org

Library of Congress Catalog Card Number: 00-108935

ISBN 1-889544-13-2

Copyright © 2000, 2002 Children's Resources International, Inc.

0320005

CRI PUBLICTAIONS

CREATING CHILD-CENTERED PROGRAMS FOR INFANTS AND TODDLERS

Caregivers learn how to design a safe, healthy, and responsive environment for infants and toddlers; how to support young children's learning; and how to staff and evaluate a child-centered program.

LEARNING ACTIVITIES FOR INFANTS AND TODDLERS:
AN EASY GUIDE FOR EVERYDAY USE

Offers caregivers more than 100 hands-on, developmentally appropriate activities that caregivers can incorporate into the child's day. Each activity includes a purpose, list of materials, and simple steps for preparation. In addition, each activity provides a "home connection," to involve parents and extend the activity at home.

CREATING CHILD-CENTERED CLASSROOMS: 3-5 YEAR OLDS

Helps teachers create active learning environments for preschool-age children, individualize teaching, and involve families in the program. Teachers learn observation techniques to teach to the strengths, interests, and needs of each child.

CREATING CHILD-CENTERED MATERIALS

Assists educators in designing and making their own classroom materials for active exploration in nine activity centers. Each activity includes a "home connection" that links the child's family to the classroom learning experiences. Easy-to-follow directions allow teachers and parents to create activities from recycled and natural materials.

CREATING INCLUSIVE CLASSROOMS

Provides the research base, practical methods and real-world case studies that guide and support teachers through issues such as family partnerships, IEP development, and adapting the classroom environment.

EDUCATION AND THE CULTURE OF DEMOCRACY

This book contends that there are subtle, yet effective teaching techniques that encourage democracy: choice, individualism, creativity, equality, respect for differences, and appreciation of individuals' needs while maintaining the balance for the greater good of the group.

For more information, contact:
Children's Resources International
5039 Connecticut Ave., NW, Suite One
Washington, DC 20008
phone: 202-363-9002/fax: 202-363-9550/info@crinter.com
www.childrensresources.org

TABLE OF CONTENTS

FOREWORD

Never doubt that a small group of thoughtful, committed citizens can change the world. Indeed, it is the only thing that ever has.

—Margaret Mead (American anthropologist)

Parents' Voices

The voices of parents need to be heard. While an increasing number of organizations speak out on behalf of children, politicians and other decision-makers need to hear *first-hand* from families about their concerns for their children's education, health care, safety, and the other significant issues that touch families' lives. Educators, school administrators, and government officials also need to hear about families' hopes and dreams for their children. When these decision-makers hear directly from parents or a parent group about seemingly small-scale concerns, such as neglected parks, dangerous street corners, and playgrounds in need of repair, these concerns take on real importance and power.

Given the power of parents' voices to influence decisions made in the public arena, it is important that more of them be heard. Unfortunately, many parents view the political system as too complex, distant, or corrupt to be influenced by their efforts. Families who feel alienated from the public systems that serve them are especially unlikely to participate in the political process. This raises the vital question: *How can parents become more involved in the decision-making processes within their neighborhoods, schools, and local governments in order to make sure their concerns for children are heard?*

The Purpose of This Book

This book is designed to provide parents and others with the skills necessary to organize effectively and speak out on issues that affect children at home, at school, and in the broader community. Advocacy, which is the ability to persuade, argue, and stand up for a cause, is the main tool that enables parents to translate their concerns into concrete actions. When combined with community

ix

action, where concerned individuals join together to address identified problems or needs, parents have at their disposal an effective and powerful set of tools for bringing about change.

The history of advocacy shows that no one speaks more effectively for children than their own parents and family members. When the voices of those most affected are developed, raised, and acted upon, communities become more vital, caring places in which to live and raise children. This book answers the important question raised above by helping parents become effective advocates in their homes, schools, and communities, as they come to believe in and feel competent exercising their rights as democratic citizens.

Making a Difference

The inspiration for this book is drawn from the experience of parents involved in Step by Step, a unique and successful early childhood education program, which serves more than 500,000 children and families and operates throughout Central and Eastern Europe, Central Asia, South Africa, and Haiti. This program introduces child-centered teaching methods in emerging democracies and supports community and family involvement in preschools and primary schools. Through participation in their children's education, Step by Step parents learned that they could make a difference and became successful advocates for their children.

Democracy provides parents and other concerned citizens with significant avenues for making concerns heard. Among the rights afforded citizens in a democracy is the right to influence the policies of the government and to elect its top decision-makers. When fully exercised, these rights give citizens significant power to affect change. Admittedly, even in democracies, some individuals exert more influence and power because of their access to resources, funding, and organizations. However, as the experience of Step by Step parents and countless other parent advocates around the world demonstrates, change has just as much to do with each citizen's desire, commitment, and ability to make his or her voice heard.

Making a Difference: A Parent's Guide to Advocacy and Community Action provides parents and other concerned citizens with concrete ideas, strategies, and action steps to turn aspirations into actions. The book presents a clear and systematic approach to advocacy and organizing, building and using the power of citizens to create communities and institutions that promote change. The format is designed with busy parents in mind. Readers can either select individual chapters of interest to them, or proceed from the beginning, "Why Take Action?" to the end, "Real-life Examples of Advocates in Action" for a more comprehensive understanding of the process of advocacy and community action. Each chapter includes key principles of advocacy and organizing, strategies for turning plans into action, advocacy and organizing examples taken from real-life, and finally, "how-to" advice for building lasting organizations for change.

Throughout, this book is filled with inspirational accounts from real-life advocates around the world, from parents to teachers, from artists to grandparents. Examples of individual, family, and community action are provided as both a foundation and springboard for action. These compelling stories are intertwined with practical advice and guidance about the basic steps of advocacy and community action. It is my hope that from these pages, parents and others who care about children will gain a voice that they can raise to make a difference.

This book, *Making a Difference: A Parent's Guide to Advocacy and Community Action*, came about as a result of contributions from many individuals. The authors, Diane J. Charnov and Carolyn Rutsch, provided their expertise in advocacy and community action and worked tirelessly to make the book easy-to-use and informative. Mike Mathers, a Step by Step teacher-trainer, enlivened the text with his creative drawings. Elisa Slattery edited the book, Cassie Marshall developed the page design and formatted the text, and the Crosby Group created the cover design. Staff at Children's Resources International—Michele Redalen, Ellen Daniels, Julie Empson, and Pam Coughlin—reviewed the book in its various iterations. I would like to express my gratitude to each of these people for their tireless effort and support.

Pam Coughlin
Children's Resources International

CHAPTER I: WHY TAKE ACTION?

Things do not get better by being left alone.

—*Winston Churchill (British Prime Minister)*

Introduction

If you are reading this, it is likely that you are someone who does not want to accept the status quo and has already identified a need that affects your child or your community. You may want to improve your child's school, and make your neighborhood safer and more welcoming to children. Or you may have a long list of concerns and are not sure where to begin. The desire to make change is important. However, desire alone is not sufficient to achieve results. This chapter and Chapter II discuss why it is important to take action. Chapters III, IV, and V provide information on where to begin and how to achieve your goals.

Why Parents Are Reluctant to Act

Many parents ask themselves, "Why should I bother to get involved? Can I really make a difference?" In many places, the way things are is the way they have always been, and to some, the way they will always be. Everywhere, parents are busy taking care of their families and children and working long and hard hours. Sometimes isolated and tired, many "make do," and become used to poor sanitation, poor schools, few rights, and limited opportunities for their children. From Azerbaijan to South Africa, when early childhood educators asked citizens about their desires for change and why they might not have taken actions in their communities, the reasons, throughout these diverse communities, sounded a common note.

1

- People are busy.
- People are shy and afraid to speak up.
- There is no "tradition" of action to follow.
- There is a lack of hope that things can be better.
- There is a lack of knowledge of rights.

When "Making Do" Won't Do

Absent resources and a tradition of activism, parents "make do" with what they have. Sometimes, in making do, people can make the best of their situations. But often, making do is a quiet acceptance of unacceptable conditions and communities may never reach their potential or may even degenerate. This situation is referred to as the "broken window" syndrome. When windows, buildings, fences, and other structures in neighborhoods remain in disrepair or are "broken," studies show that a dilapidated, external community appearance contributes to the legitimacy and acceptance of poor services. Simply put, at some point, no one cares when a neighborhood has broken windows, trash on the street, and rusty playground equipment. Left to linger, this seeming lack of care for buildings can translate into a lack of caring in a community.

Dare to Dream

One neighborhood in Massachusetts (U.S.A.) held a contest, centered around the American civil rights leader Martin Luther King's "I Have a Dream" theme. They asked children to draw pictures of the kinds of communities they would like to live in and imagine better playgrounds, nicer schools, and safer streets. A few entries were selected and local artists painted these dreams on advertising space in the downtown area. This was one way to give concrete, visual direction to imagination and hope. Of course, advocacy and commitment

are both necessary to turn these dreams into reality, but identifying goals is a critical first step in the whole process. If the status quo is not the way you want things to be, then dare to dream. Ask yourself:

- Am I satisfied with the way things are?
- Is this what I want for myself, my family, and my community?

If your answer is, "No, I want more, I wish for a better life for myself, my family, and my community," then it's time to move beyond your dreams and:

✢ Identify your needs
✢ Develop a course of action

What Do I Want to Achieve?
Your dreams can be a starting point. After that, it is time to move beyond the thinking stage and turn your motivations into actions. Clearly identifying the specific steps that need to be addressed early on will help ensure your efforts have the best chance for success. The steps that follow are suggestions and examples to answer the important question, "Where do I begin if I want to make improvements in my community?"

Make a community needs inventory. The first step is to take a community inventory of areas that fall short of your expectations. Make a list. Write down your wishes for a better community. Think about your child's school, from the quality of the education to the number of students in a classroom. Think about the availability of community services, from library materials to sanitation services. What falls short of your expectations? This is the time when you can "dare to dream," and imagine the ideal school or community for you and your child.

The following is an example of a list of needs you might create:

- The community playground is littered with trash and broken glass.
- Parents want a cleaner, safe environment for children and families to play in.
- Lunches provided by the school lack the nutritional value needed by children.
- The school does not have basic classroom supplies. There is no school library.
- At recess, there is no sports equipment for the children.
- Students are in danger because cars are going too fast in front of the elementary school.
- Pet owners are not cleaning up after their pets.

When you write your list of needs and concerns, organize your concerns broadly. Consider all areas of your daily life, from safety issues to health concerns, to community spirit. Think about your child's classroom and school. Review the conditions of the streets and buildings you and your family frequent, as well as parks where your children play on the weekends. You may even want to carry a small notebook with you for a week and write down your concerns when you confront them. Some questions you might ask about your school include:

- Are supplies adequate? Are there enough educational materials, as well as physical supplies?
- Does the local school accommodate people who speak different languages? Are key holidays celebrated by a community's minority religious and ethnic groups recognized on the school calendar? Are those days acknowledged when scheduling tests, performances, and school days?
- Are educational resources adequate? Is the student-teacher ratio sufficient?
- Are the needs of children with disabilities (educational, health) being met?

Other questions you might want to ask about your community include:

- Are the physical structures of public institutions adequate? Are sidewalks "walk-able," buildings and parks clean and functioning?
- Are services adequate for a wide variety of people in the community?

- Are services flexible? Do library hours meet the needs of parents' work and children's school schedules?

This is only a sample of issues that affect communities. Each community has its own set of specific needs. When drawing up your community-based needs list, take into account those issues that apply to you and may be unique to families in your community.

Am I the Only One With This Concern?
People who live near each other, participate in the same activities, attend the same schools and religious institutions, and even walk the same streets are likely to share concerns. You may be surprised to find that your list contains many of the

same issues as those of your neighbors, co-workers, and friends. Of course, some problems and needs may be unique to you. If that is the case, the information provided in this manual will enable you to successfully pursue a "go-it-alone" strategy. There are a number of situations where your concern is a legitimate one, but others do not have the same motivation to act. In that case, you will still need to perform the same steps as outlined for group action that are discussed throughout this book, but instead of seeking community support, you will need to focus on identifying the proper decision-makers and maintaining your personal motivation.

Evaluate Your List of Community Needs
Now that you have identified your issues, the next step is to evaluate them. Some issues are better candidates for action than others. One way to tell if your issue is a good candidate for community action is to consider if it has some of the following qualities. Three questions to help you evaluate your list are:

Is change possible? Don't choose such an overwhelming problem that the likelihood of change is remote. You may not be able to overhaul an entire school system, but there are improvements that can be made in your child's classroom. Your cause should be *achievable*, as best as you can determine at the outset, and the impact should be *measurable*.

> You can't roll up your sleeves and get to work if you are wringing your hands.

Does your concern have the makings of a "winnable" case? Is there some chance for success? Is there some hope of gain? Is it manageable in scope? Nothing breeds success like success. An initial "win" will help maintain motivation to continue to seek further improvements.

Do others in my community share this concern? Is it a need that is widely felt and affects many? Is it a need that is deeply felt and has a strong emotional or human element? There is comfort in numbers. The more people are affected and the more deeply they are moved, the more likely they will be to commit themselves to a cause.

The last question, "Do others in my community share my concern?" may be the most important one to reflect upon. One feature of an issue that is well-suited to group advocacy is that it touches many people's lives and can draw upon the resources and skills of others in your community. There is a saying, "You can't roll up your sleeves and get to work if you are wringing your hands." As you move from the "thinking" phase into the "acting" phase, keep this in mind. It may help inspire a shift from *worrying* about a problem to *doing* something about it.

Chapter I: Why Take Action?

At this stage you should have:

✤ Prepared a list of community needs
✤ Narrowed the list to identify problems that are community based, touch many people's lives, are achievable, and have measurable results

Your Role in Achieving Your Goals
Now is the time to actively outline your role in achieving your goals. One stumbling block some people encounter is that they don't think they can make a difference. Before you get stuck in the rut of "I can't" or "someone else is better qualified than me to take action," remember that some of the most important qualities needed to make a difference are:

• Commitment
• Perseverance
• Communication skills

Your talents. If you think you "can't," reconsider. List the positive qualities you possess. Everyone possesses talents. Good advocates take advantage of their strengths. Well-organized action groups seek individuals with a wide range of talents. Just as you assessed your community needs, it is also important to make a personal skills inventory. List your strengths, talents, and life experiences that will help support your goals for improving your community. You may be surprised to discover that as you review your own life experiences your talents are greater than you think. You likely have a wealth of hidden talents that are essential ingredients in a recipe for community action and involvement.

> If you can walk you can dance. If you can talk, you can sing.
>
> Zimbabwe Proverb

There is an old Zimbabwe proverb, "If you can walk, you can dance. If you can talk, you can sing." Simple daily life experiences are often overlooked assets. They can provide a strong foundation for building community advocacy skills.

One's own steps in life can be the source of community partnerships and advocacy skills. When paired with other people, simple steps, taken together can become a "dance," for the good of the community.

Have you ever? Then you can. As you prepare your personal assets list, look at the following and see which experiences describe you best. Add your own "life experiences" to the list and then imagine how these hidden talents could make you well-suited to community action. Have you ever...?:

- Organized a birthday party for children, an anniversary celebration for parents, a meeting?
- Helped a neighbor paint, take out trash, or lent a tool?
- Enjoyed a sport, hobby, or recipe and shared it with others?
- Brought food to a potluck dinner?
- Spoke up when you received the wrong change, saw someone throw trash on the ground?
- Shoveled the snow from a sidewalk beyond the boundaries of your home?

Applying your skills. If you recognize yourself in any of these situations, from lending books to helping a neighbor shovel a sidewalk, then you probably help in the community more than you realize. Seeing yourself as a "doer," and recognizing yourself as a "community helper" is one step toward applying your skills toward new goals. Skills used in organizing family gatherings are also used in advocacy. The experiences of performing functions, like preparing party lists (deciding who to invite), and assigning tasks (deciding who brings what meal to a potluck), are all part of the organizational process (identifying needs and assigning tasks), which is critical to success of action groups.

- *If you have close friends*, then you already have a community of people who you can use as a base. Your skills as a good friend, from being a good listener to being someone who can be trusted with information, can also be used by an action group. Good listeners make for good note-takers at meetings where accuracy is important. Trust developed from years of friendships can be useful in media contacts as you honestly answer questions.

- *If you have given away clothes* your family has outgrown or passed along books when you finished reading them, these same needs you have filled with friends and family can be organized on a larger scale. You could establish a lending library at a local school or a clothing exchange in the community.

> Use what talents you possess. The woods would be very silent if no birds sang there except those that sang the best.

- *If you have ever tried something new*, taken a new class, learned another language, tried a new recipe, then you are *flexible* and *willing to try new things*. These qualities will serve you well as you strike out to improve life in your community.

- *If you have watched a neighbor's child* for an afternoon, then you have put someone's needs in your community ahead of your own. You might consider organizing with other parents in the neighborhood to establish a baby-sitting cooperative that would accommodate many parents' work schedules.

Even if you have never done any of these things, your unique network of personal relations provides a base for community skills. As a daughter or son, parent, or grandparent, you have long been involved in a community, working together to achieve goals. Family relationships have prepared you for taking an active part in a community beyond that of relatives. Your personal experiences, whether gained through your family or work experiences, can be a strong foundation for community action.

Why Parents Make Good Advocates

Sometimes people want to go to "experts" to solve problems. Certainly, there are times when that is necessary. But, in the case of advocacy and action, parents are often their children's first and best advocates. Parents are the "experts" because they possess:

- *First-hand knowledge* of a child's or children's needs. Parents are best qualified to know their children's needs. Just as parents can distinguish a child's cry of pain from one of hunger, they can also tell the difference between a child who is somewhat upset and one who is seriously ill.

- *Dedication and motivation to act.* It is the parent and the child who are most affected when needs go unmet in a community. For instance, a parent of a special needs child brings a special kind of caring and the extra dedication necessary to improving services for children.

- *Credibility.* Decision-makers are more likely to listen to parents than third-party "spokespersons" who dispassionately relay problems. Lawmakers can be moved by strong, human stories. When told directly by those most affected, the facts are likely to be told most accurately and the impact can be a strong motivator for change.

How Your Family and the Community Benefit from Your Action

While parents often make the best advocates for their children, they might not always be aware of their rights or recognize their potential in fulfilling this role. This book will help make parents more aware of their rights as well as provide them with the "how-to" skills necessary to seek change. When a community bands together to take action, parents, children, and the community as a whole can benefit.

Parents become:
- Aware and informed
- Confident about their abilities
- Cognizant of their own needs and those of others
- Able to speak up for what they believe is important
- Informed about the "system" and develop skills to take action
- Connected to a more caring community
- Models of civic action for their families

The Community:
- Gains an enhanced quality of life
- Achieves greater participation from its citizens
- Realizes increased connections among citizens through growing community spirit
- Accomplishes a sense of community ownership
- Acquires a safer environment and enhanced community services

The Children:
- Gain new pride in knowing their parents and their community care
- Learn key lessons in how to become active citizen participants when they grow up
- Obtain improved services, from better educational opportunities to a safer community
- Feel an increased sense of caring from their community
- Realize better opportunities for a healthier, safer upbringing

Advocacy is a process that involves many steps. This chapter has focused on the initial steps of:

- Identifying one's concerns
- Identifying one's own skills and strengths
- Understanding why parents make good advocates
- Understanding how a community benefits from advocacy actions

Chapter II takes off from this starting point with a series of specific suggestions for how to achieve your goals. Through examples and case studies, the next chapter shows how to turn "what-ifs" into "how-tos" and explains how advocacy actions can be used to make changes in your life and your community.

CHAPTER II: GETTING STARTED

Life is a journey, not a destination.

Steps for Advocating

This chapter is designed to *clarify* further steps needed to put the process of advocacy into practice. It seeks to illustrate the process of advocacy with case-studies based on real-life situations. In so doing, it will help build skills to enable parents and other concerned citizens to become advocates and improve their communities. Specifically, this chapter will provide examples on how to:

Step 1:
Determine your goal

Step 2:
Review your goal

Step 3:
Gather facts

Step 4:
Develop action strategies

Step 5:
Identify key decision-makers

✛ Determine goals
✛ Gather facts
✛ Develop short- and long-term action strategies
✛ Identify key decision-makers
✛ Determine whether to "go it alone" or join an existing group

The saying, "Life is a journey, not a destination," applies especially well to advocacy. It expresses the idea that one's destination is not the only goal. Rather, the process of the journey is equally if not more important. Advocacy, like an eagerly awaited trip, entails many steps and it has intermediate and ultimate destinations and goals. Those who enjoy outings, whether a school field trip, a visit to relatives, or a simple hike in the woods, know that travel requires preparation, organization, planning and choosing a desirable destination, and packing appropriate supplies. The following is a road map designed to outline the steps for those who travel the advocacy road.

Step 1: Determine your goal or what you want to achieve.
On any journey, a traveler undertakes a series of steps to make sure the experience is rewarding. Preparation for a journey includes choosing an interesting destination (the goal or ultimate aim), learning about a region (gathering facts), assessing the terrain and the route (determining action strategies), deciding whether to travel alone (individual action) or bring companions (group action). The first step on the journey is to decide what you want to achieve or your goal. If your concern is the poor nutritional quality of food at your child's school, your goal might be to get more nutritious lunches served on a regular basis. The next step is to make sure that your goal is important and potentially achievable.

Step 2: Review your goal.
What makes for a good family trip also makes for a good advocacy journey. Reviewing your goal, and asking, "Is this an important issue?" is similar to asking your family, "where should we go?" on a family outing. Parents traveling with children often report that they enjoyed the trip more if they chose an interesting destination and took into account the ages of their children and their temperaments and interests. Similarly, when choosing an advocacy goal and identifying a community need, parents need to be equally attentive to all aspects of the trip, especially the destination (goal).

For first-time advocates, small-scale objectives may be the best way to get started. Just as the first-time traveler may choose to stay close to home, the first-time advocate may prefer to take on an issue that is small in scope so as to practice new skills. In some situations, a trial run is a good way to hone communication and organizational skills, and practice shaping an effective message and recruiting supporters. And, if the first attempt is not a success, a small issue is also a small loss. Parents should consider whether the objective is well-suited to their situation and strengths. To determine whether the goal is a good match with your skills and strengths and those of your partners, use the following checklist. Ask if the goal or aim is:

- Widely felt?
- Supported by evidence?
- Suited to your skills?
- Likely to succeed?

If the answer to most of the above is more likely "yes" than "no," then you are ready to proceed with the next step of uncovering evidence to support your cause.

Step 3: Gather facts

Facts are critical to answering your questions, "What do I want to accomplish? What do I want to change?" Facts are also essential to answering questions from decision-makers and potential supporters whom you will need to convince. Investing time and energy in gathering facts is important. It helps build a foundation for a strong case and solidifies your reputation as a reliable advocate.

Facts can help:
- Clarify the problem
- Develop a strategy and articulate goals
- Shape a message
- Reach and define an intended audience

The first-time advocate may wonder:
- "Where do I go to get my facts?"
- "Where do I find evidence supporting my cause?"
- "How do I know if others share my concern?"

Sources for research may be as close as your own home or neighborhood. Talk with your children about their school, chat with a neighbor about the community, read the local paper, and attend school meetings. These are all simple ways to

One neighborhood used the "Letter to the Editor" section to build community support and save a local park from destruction. Many who had not previ-ously known about the problem heard the public appeal. This simple start-ing point, a letter from a concerned citizen, proved to be the catalyst for community action.

stay informed about your community and help you "do your homework." For instance, when you read the local paper you might find a "Letter to the Editor" on an issue of personal concern (such as the local park). You can even put an ad in the paper asking if there are others who share your concern. Follow up. Contact the writer who shares your concern. Doing research is easier than you might think. It can involve:

- First-hand observation (walk to school with your child)
- Formal and informal conversations (talk to neighbors to see if they share your concern)
- Newspaper and media research (read the paper, look at "Letters to the Editor")
- Local hearings and school board meetings (attend meetings on issues of interest)

Something as simple as a chat with a neighbor may reveal that others share your concerns (about the speed of traffic near school or lack of supplies). When you stay abreast of court decisions or listen to the news, you may find that decisions regarding people with disabilities, zoning, or school issues may be useful to your case.

Observe a situation first-hand. Listen to your child ("What are her concerns?"). Observe a classroom ("I see there are not enough chairs for everyone to do a project at the same time"). Attend school and neighborhood meetings, read the newspaper, talk with a neighbor. These are all ways to gather facts that apply to your situation. While trips to the library or conversations with neighbors are useful, in some cases, first-hand research is even more important.

Chapter II: Getting Started

Parents around the world have long pleaded with their children, "Do your homework." When you plan your advocacy "assignment," remember an effective advocate is also someone who does her homework. A successful advocate often goes beyond the textbook and does additional research. Sometimes, you may need to do some footwork as well to gather facts. What follows are three examples of how effective footwork can be.

Parents "Count"

In one community, parents knew of many Spanish-speaking children in an English-language school. Even so, the local school did not offer any special services to these children. A group of parents took it upon themselves to obtain increased language services for their children. They went door-to-door, equipped only with pencil, paper, and determination, and counted the number of children who spoke Spanish as their primary language and lived in the school district. With the new data, the group approached the school board. The data and the parents' determination made for a strong case. The school board decided to increase services to Spanish-speaking families. Spanish-language books were added in the school library, neighborhood residents were recruited as bilingual teachers, and English as a Second Language (ESL) classes were added.

How Loud Is Too Loud? or, In Search of Peace and Quiet

In another case, a neighborhood was bothered by the constant noise of a local highway. Years of letter writing, homeowner meetings, and appointments with local officials had not been fruitful. Ultimately, one homeowner bought an inexpensive decibel level meter and took the time to go out every morning and evening to objectively measure the noise level in front of local homes. With that information recorded, the community was able to show that there was severe noise pollution. Evidence of high decibel level readings was presented to decision-makers along with testimony from audiologists and pediatricians that sustained exposure to such loud noises could be harmful to young children. Noise barriers were erected in the community to dampen the sound of traffic. The quiet restored to the neighborhood added to the sense of peace and enabled families to enjoy their homes more.

Food Allergies: The Peanut Case

One family had recently moved from a school district where there were no special procedures in place for her child with a severe and life-threatening allergy to peanuts. In the new school, the parent was determined to help her son. Before the child's first day, she contacted the principal and homeroom teacher to inform  them about the situation. She presented journal articles that documented the prevalence and severity of food allergies in children. She went door to door asking parents about their children's allergies and found that others suffered from this same problem. The parent's ability to calmly provide accurate information set the stage for a solution. Working together, the parent and teacher posted "No Peanut Zone" signs inside and outside the classroom. The picture of a peanut with a big slash across the shell told the story to the young children. The words, "No Peanut Zone," written in many languages, alerted the diverse group of multilingual parents and older children. An information sheet about the severity of the allergy was also given to parents. This problem was successfully addressed through a series of simple yet effective actions because the parent advocate did her homework and her footwork.

As the preceding examples show, the likelihood of persuading others to share your concern and do something about a situation is heightened when your facts are:

- Accurate
- Compelling
- Calmly articulated

As a parent, you are best qualified to understand the situation and need. Your first-hand knowledge and deep interest in the cause will serve you well. But, in addition to passion and commitment, objective facts are essential to preparing a good case for advocacy. At first, your desire to act may have been driven by emotions. You might have said, "It makes me so mad that the children don't have recess because there are no balls to play with!" or been angry and said, "I can't believe that there are no after-school facilities for children since most parents work so late." But, sustained interest in an issue and the involvement of others depends on a broad base of objective facts rather than emotions.

Step 4: Develop short- and long-term action strategies

Just as you might plot out different routes to reach a destination, it is also wise to have different routes on your advocacy journey. Now that you have gathered your facts, it is time to assess the terrain of your issue. Ask, "What are the roadblocks? What are the resources? How do I draw up a plan of action?" The answers will vary depending on the situation, the community, the resources, and other factors. Sometimes parents need to come up with an immediate solution (highway route) to a serious problem endangering their children like in the case of the peanut allergy. Other times, a longer-term solution (scenic route) is required. Often, a combination of both approaches is needed. The following examples illustrate how short- and long-term action strategies can work in tandem.

Cars and Kids

One problem common in many communities is that children are at risk because of cars speeding by where children walk to school or play. The hazard comes from a combination of factors. Because children are short they are not always visible to drivers. Because children often move quickly, darting in a street to chase after a lost ball, they are at risk. Adults are often

in a hurry, rushing to work and errands. These factors converge to create hazardous situations. The following shows how the combination of short- and long-term strategies can help deal with both the immediate problem and the chronic situation. In the case of speeding in a local neighborhood, one man in the community, a painter, put up a sign that said, "Slow Down" after a near miss involving his daughter. A concerned neighbor who was not a parent, placed a brightly colored "speed cone" in the street with "Slow" painted on it. Another community member placed a notice in the local newsletter describing the many near misses in the neighborhood and expressed her concerns about the children's safety and that local citizens could be party to a tragedy if drivers didn't slow down. One teacher who lived in the neighborhood designed a safety program at school. She initiated a series of classroom discussions about the importance of "Stop, Look, and Listen" before entering a street, used a puppet named "Bike-Well Bear," to emphasize the importance of bike safety to children, and brought in a local safety patrol to school to discuss road safety with the children.

The problem of speeding cars near children underscores the benefits of a *two-pronged approach*. The *short-term*, immediate strategy to address a safety hazard was to notify the community via obvious signs in the road. The *longer-term* strategy was to use existing mechanisms (neighborhood news) and appeal to parents' concerns about their children's welfare as well as their own and to work jointly with existing institutions (the local school) to teach children about safety issues.

Community Mentoring

In a city plagued by long-standing economic and social problems, the community came together to hold a "Community Pride Day." This celebration (short-term, immediate reward) paved the way for future contacts. In time, this short-term approach led to more long-term strategies for dealing with ingrained problems. A "Mentor" system was created, pairing young boys with older community members willing to help with after-school homework to work on, improving the children's reading skills, and to offer friendship. Starting small, fixing one "broken" window at a time, can be an important first step in bringing a community together to address more fundamental, structural concerns.

The Case of the Dirty Park

The following is an example that illustrates the effectiveness of combining short- and long-term action strategies. This case revolves around another "universal" problem shared by neighborhoods worldwide. Often, parks are neither as clean nor as safe as parents would like. In one community, the local park was the only free space available to community residents to relax outdoors. Unfortunately, it was dirty and run-down.

A short-term strategy was to organize a "Clean-Up Day" to rehabilitate the park and give it a new "look." As an enticement to draw support, notices were placed on bulletin boards in the community and flyers were sent home from school, announcing a picnic for those who helped beautify the park.

Community members knew that the situation needed more than a "one-time fix." The park needed maintenance on an ongoing basis. "Clean-Up Day" was a temporary solution to an ongoing problem. To address the chronic nature of the situation, a few concerned parents worked with the school. The local school was a natural partner since it was near the park the school children would benefit most from its use. The school sponsored an "Adopt-a-Park" program. On a regularly scheduled basis, the school organized "Park Beautification Days," planted

shrubs and flowers (donated by a local nursery), threw away garbage, and made signs recognizing the school and its sponsors (advertising for local businesses).

Teachers became involved and integrated the park activities into their educational program in the school science unit. Children studied nature and the growth process through their involvement in planting in the park. Seedlings were grown and observed in the classroom and then transferred to the parkland. Children earned "points" for community service that could be applied to their school grades. The whole neighborhood benefited. In the short term, "Clean-Up Day" was important to boost morale and energize others around an issue. In the long run, using the park as a resource for teaching science was beneficial educationally. The immediate gratification of the "Clean-Up Day" picnic was a fun and easy "reward" to those who offered their support. It also helped bring the community together, an important element in organizing future activities.

Step 5: Identify key decision-makers

Decision-makers are people too. These people of "influence" might be your neighbors, parents of your children's friends, or users of your same local services (libraries, parks, grocery stores). They may be more approachable than you think. Effective advocates use common bonds to their advantage. By talking with your neighbors you might discover that one of your own friends knows a local official. Or, you might find that the woman down the street sits on a local school board. One neighborhood mother was surprised to discover that her neighbor of many years was a retired school principal. When the family was experiencing school-related problems, this friend and former school principal was able to intervene and mediate the situation.

After an advocate has selected an issue of concern, gathered the relevant facts, and devised long- and short-term strategies, the next ingredient essential to a good advocacy plan revolves around the question,

✢ "What do I do with the information?"
✢ "Who should be made aware of these facts?"

Which decision-maker you choose to approach is based on the type of problem or need you have identified. For instance, if the situation is school-based, the relevant decision-maker may be a(n):

- Classroom teacher
- School principal
- Resource teacher
- School nurse, nutritionist, counselor.
- Parent on the Parent Teacher Association or Organization (PTA, PTO, or similar group)
- Elected school board official

If the issue is related to your neighborhood, or the community at large, a problem with street lights, crime, or even trash removal, relevant decision-makers may be a:

- Neighborhood Association member
- Local government official
- Representative from the mayor's office
- Library board member

Your ability to identify the appropriate decision-makers in your case is important for many reasons. It can play a part in how you structure your message or affect the timing of its delivery. If the decision-making body you need to reach is a school, town, or board, it is important to:

- Know when the board meets (weekly, monthly, or quarterly).
- Understand the process of airing your concern.
- Know how to get your issue on the agenda. Do you submit a letter in writing? By what date? Do you attend an open meeting with a prepared statement?
- Get a list of board members, and draft and distribute a sample letter.

Lending Library

Knowing who is "in charge" may determine how you shape your message. Perhaps your issue involves expanding community-based services, such as those at a local library. By targeting decision-makers (in this case, the library board), one community was able to increase the availability of several newspapers to its readers on a daily basis. By understanding the board's process, presenting concerns directly to the board, getting on their agenda, and following the board's rules, the community was able to keep its citizens better informed. In another case, one library expanded its lending services from books to tools. Using library cards, community members were able to check out tools to help rebuild a community hurt by natural disaster. Knowledge of the process and a few willing citizens led to a significant improvement.

> A man who goes alone can start today, but he who travels with another must wait till the other is ready.
>
> Henry David Thoreau, American writer and philosopher

Individual Action

Advocacy is a potent tool that can be used by individuals as well as groups to effect change. When you embark on a journey, there are times you may want to bring along companions, and times when you may want to go it alone. One hallmark of democracy is the ability of a single individual to make a profound difference. Situations will arise where a cause is valid and important, but it is also highly personal. Perhaps the issue applies only to your family, or you may be the only family in your area with a child who requires special services, or the only house on a corner littered with trash. In situations like these, all the strategies for group action outlined in this manual apply equally well to individuals who want to take action.

Ramps in School
One family found their child was the only wheel-chair user in the community. In this case, it was not possible to form an action group.   Therefore, the child's parents became the sole, but still highly effective, advocate for their child. They were able to get ramps in the school to allow their child to go from class to class like his friends. Joining class-mates in all the activities of the day made a big dif-ference in the child's attitude toward school.

This chapter started parents on the road to advocacy. When parents apply these five steps toward achieving their advocacy goals, whether in groups or on their own, they will likely become more comfortable approaching power figures and voicing their concerns. Ultimately, when the tool of advocacy is applied, power relationships can become more democratic and just and communities can become healthier, safer, and more productive places to live. Now that you have begun the journey, the next chapter is designed to provide concrete assistance in moving you along the advocacy path.

CHAPTER III: REACHING OUT AND INVOLVING OTHERS

A community flourishes when its citizens plant trees under whose shade they will never sit.

Ancient Greek Saying

Ideally, the sentiments expressed in the ancient Greek saying, "A community flourishes when its citizens plant trees under whose shade they will never sit," would be apparent in all communities. In reality, competing interests, lack of time, or just lack of practice in group efforts hampers progress and change. Even if the motivation to help exists, there may not always be the resources or the know-how to "plant trees" (do good work) for the benefit of others.

This chapter and Chapter IV provide practical advice to help parents reach out, involve others, and make a difference in their communities. These pages will help answer questions like, "How do I *find* an action group?" and "How do I *form* one?" Read as one unit, Chapters III, IV, and V will provide the tools necessary to accomplish your goals as an advocate. At this point in the journey, you should have identified:

✤ Key community concerns
✤ Personal skills and strengths
✤ Compelling facts
✤ Your advocacy goals and strategies
✤ Relevant decision-maker(s)

While there is no one route to advocacy that can take into account all the different "trips" to be undertaken, there are common situations all advocates may encounter. The following questions are designed to help guide any advocacy traveler. They include:

- Do I need support?
- What are the benefits of involving others?
- Where do I turn for support?
- What if none exists?

Do I Need Support?

In the classic children's book, *Alice's Adventures Underground*, a sequel to the better known, *Alice in Wonderland*, Alice shrinks in size after drinking a strange liquid and worries that she will drown in a sea of her own tears. With the help of her friends, Alice escapes this fate and emerges taller and stronger into the world. Lewis Carroll's nineteenth century heroine is relevant to the experiences of a twenty-first century advocacy traveler. Facing new situations and undertaking change is often, *but not always*, more than a one-person job. Gathering support along the way can help:

> "I wish I hadn't cried so much!" said Alice, as she swam about, trying to find her way out. I shall be punished for it now, I suppose, by being drowned in my own tears!"
>
> Lewis Carroll,
> *Alice's Adventures Underground*

- Overcome individual weaknesses
- Pool people's talents
- Bring a community closer together by defining similar goals

Reaching out and involving others in an advocacy journey is like adding partners on a trip. In the case of advocacy, the supplies are *knowledge, skills,* and *energy,* all of which help make a journey rewarding and productive. Groups benefit when they take advantage of a wide range of individual contributions rather than seek carbon-copy members. Groups that seek only like-minded members may suffer from a deficit of skills and ideas. Parents and educators recognize that children bring into this world their own unique talents; similarly, when organizing advocacy groups, adults too bring a varied set of skills and contributions to society. Complementary skills and diverse personality types are invaluable to a well-run group. Strong groups draw from a broad array of people with complementary skills, from outgoing speakers to talented writers, to innovative artists and bakers. The following examines some of the benefits that accrue when a diverse group of individuals join together to make a difference.

What Are the Benefits of Involving Others?
The benefits of involving others can be compared to the difference between a snowflake and a snowstorm, a trickle of water and a stream. The raw material is the same, but the sheer mass makes a significant difference in terms of impact. Similarly, well-run groups, mobilized around important issues, can accomplish many things. Community action can:

Win real, immediate, concrete improvements in people's lives. An action group can make real gains for large numbers of people. These improvements can make a big difference in people's lives, from providing more nutritious school lunches, to rejuvenating parks and neighborhoods for children, to removing lead paint in neighborhood housing.

Give people a sense of their own power. Community action groups involve a group of citizens working together. The cooperation forged by individual issues strengthens the fabric of a community as a whole. It provides people with a sense of their own power, which is an important goal in its own right. People who exercise power on behalf of a community are then better able to exercise power on their own behalf, lobbying for better working conditions or pay raises, seeking higher degrees, and encouraging their children to speak out and do something positive for their family and community.

Alter the relations of power. Citizen advocacy and action are critical elements in sustaining a viable democracy. The building of strong, lasting organizations alters the relations of power in a community. When a group becomes strong enough, other people take it into consideration when making decisions. Action groups that are democratic in structure help make a political system work. They give voice to people who otherwise might not have been heard. Skills learned in building an advocacy organization are important, from knowing how to gather facts to how to enlist community support. Actions taken by a group help ensure its growth which ultimately helps it maintain a presence and power in the community.

> It is better to solve problems than crises.
>
> John Guinther, American writer

Benefit the next generation. Children benefit when parents actively participate in their lives as advocates. They benefit in absolute terms (better education, safer playgrounds) and abstract ways (heightened self-confidence) when parents become more involved in their community. As parents become leaders in their children's eyes, the opportunity for parent-child interaction increases. When parents gain confidence in using their new advocacy skills, children also learn critical skills. Even if a group doesn't ultimately "win" its entire cause, the process itself is important. Reared in a world where parents are "advocates," children are more likely to take up a similarly active role when they grow up.

Where Do I Turn for Support?

In the first stages of advocacy, you did your "homework" and your "footwork" to gather the facts. Now, it is time again to exercise these same skills and gather knowledge about groups and resources that exist in your community. At this stage, identifying those groups that can assist with your cause is just as important as pinpointing your needs was at the outset of the journey. Careful research at this stage will be time well spent in the long run and conserve your energy for future issues. Before you form your own action group, consider whether there are already partners in your community to turn to for support. There is no need to retrace steps others have taken. To locate sources of support and move along your advocacy journey, consider the following steps.

Classify your issue. To help you decide where to turn for support, first, identify and classify your issue. The answer, to some extent, will help determine whether an advocacy group already exists to address your needs. To classify your issue, ask whether it falls into the category of a(n):

- Public works issue (streets, neighborhoods, playgrounds)
- Educational issue (classrooms, schools, after-school care)
- Health issue (nutrition, special needs)

How you answer this question, to some extent, will shape your search.

Use community information tools. In reaching out and involving others to find support, think broadly. How did you classify your issue? What was the main subject? Just as we encourage our children to use research tools, like dictionaries and encyclopedias, to do their homework, parent advocates also need to use their community's research tools to gather information about available resources, including:

- Classroom lists
- Directories
- Phone books
- Bulletin boards

To see if a group exists that will address your needs, look through directories that may be at your library. Frequent areas where parents and children gather. Scan the local bulletin boards. Read community-based publications. Contact a teacher you like and see if she knows of a group that might address your concerns. If the

situation is health related, call the local hospital, ask a family nurse or doctor, and see if there is a support group. If the problem is in your neighborhood, before you form your own "Neighborhood Watch" organization, find out if one already exists. If the situation is school-based, work with the Parent Association and see if it can offer assistance. Sometimes, you will find that a group exists that matches your concerns. Other times, the groups or the tools to locate them are simply not there. In that case, you may need to build them yourself as the following example shows.

Directory Assistance

In many situations, the first question is, "How do I get in touch with others to raise my concerns?" Sometimes, all that is needed is a guide to help you and a way to contact the appropriate people. Having a directory (classroom, school, neighborhood, sports teams, etc.) is a key tool. In one school, no one had ever taken the time to put together a list of children and parents. Many thought that a list would soon be outdated and a "waste of time" because people moved in and out of the area on a frequent basis. Ironically, it was this very lack of contact and perceived lack of cohesion that contributed to frequent change. A few committed parents organized to make a directory. They worked with their Parent Teacher Association (PTA) to sponsor an art contest for children to design the cover and illustrate class pages. This simple contest generated community enthusiasm. Local businesses awarded free ice cream to the winners and the posters of all the entrants were hung in the halls, enlivening the dreary classroom corridors. When the directory was published, families had a way to communicate with each other. Classroom parents found it an invaluable tool in organizing field trips and special outings, and planning celebrations. This simple directory became a basic building block in knitting the community more closely together.

Use community resources. When you ask, "Where do I turn for support?" sometimes the answer will be to groups that have already been formed and other times you will be approaching new partners. Consider all the possibilities as you seek out your community resources. Start with friends and neighbors and then go further. Ask, "What are the resources that are special in my community and how might they be matched to serve the needs of families and children in my town?" Look for support from different sectors in your community. A few possibilities include public and private institutions, such as:

- Hospitals
- Religious institutions
- Universities, community colleges, and technical institutes
- Libraries and bookstores
- Museums
- Local businesses
- Service organizations
- Associations for attorneys, teachers, lobbyists, labor unions, and youth groups
- Media

Does your religious institution offer meeting space? Does a local hospital offer parent training for physical therapy needs of children? Would a nearby community college "lend" teachers-in-training to help in your school? Would a museum provide artists to assist with the art curriculum? Would a community bookstore start a young readers group after school? The following cases show how partnerships can benefit an entire community when advocates think creatively. It also shows how some advocates answered the question, "Where do I turn for support?" when they thought in unique and interesting ways.

A "Building" Museum "Builds" Community Ties

A local teacher was frustrated with her students' poor math skills. The mathematics textbook examples seemed of little interest to the children. Thinking creatively, she approached a nearby museum dedicated to the mission of architecture and building. She learned that the museum had its own problems. Though it housed fine art, its membership was dwindling and it did not attract many visitors. Museum staff, local artists, and elementary school teachers decided to join together to teach basic building skills to children. Through hands-on building projects, basic math skills were reinforced and community spirit was rejuvenated. The museum paired artists with neighborhood schools, provided supplies, including hammers, plywood, and nails, and held weekend workshops for children to learn how to construct model houses. The skills the children acquired in a

museum setting enhanced their understanding of math by using equations to solve building problems. Press coverage added publicity and awareness of the museum's good works and attendance rose. This partnership also inspired some artists to open their own studio doors to community children who were coming home to empty houses since their parents were working late. The mentor relationships that formed were important to the children, some of whom became studio assistants. The museum also benefited. Parents, some of whom had never been to a museum, became frequent visitors when their children participated in weekend workshops. Younger siblings also learned by tagging along with their older brothers and sisters. And, basic skills, like how to hammer, repair tiles, and do brickwork were important skills children used later in life as they helped with repairs on their homes and other buildings in their communities.

A Musician "Orchestrates" a Solution

In one town, the problem was a cutback in funding for music in the school budget. Parents wondered, "Where do we turn now that the school board has cut the budget for weekly music in the school?" Faced with cuts that would affect the school band, a few parents sought advice from musician friends. These part-time musicians contacted a local music store that would also face losses (from lost revenue on instrument rentals) if the school band were disbanded. One of the store's music teachers knew many of the children who would be affected. She decided to donate her teaching services in the school to keep the band going. The good will generated in parents and students alike increased the store's business, kept music in the schools, and enabled children to remain engaged in a productive pursuit that so many enjoyed.

Help From a Hospital

One boy faced a problem with social isolation due to his need to use a wheelchair in school. At first, his parents did not know where to turn. After speaking with a health-care worker, they became aware of a hospital that offered support classes for families of children with disabilities. Through the support group, the parents learned of another family with a similar situation and a solution. The boy was unable to eat lunch with his classmates because the lunchroom tables did not accommodate the dimensions of his wheelchair. Already feeling isolated by the wheelchair, the boy was especially upset when he could not eat lunch with his classmates. The solution was to build a new table that would allow wheelchair and non-wheelchair students to use the same table. Concerned families got together and built a table that would seat the boy and his friends. Just being able to sit with friends at lunch improved the boy's outlook on school.

Pursue community partnerships with existing groups. Partnerships with others in your community, both individuals and groups, can be a valuable way to accelerate the attention your cause receives. Once you have found a group with shared interests, consider whether joining it will be beneficial. Some of the steps that can help in your decision-making process include:

- Attend group meetings.
- Contact the chairperson of the group for a private discussion.
- Talk informally with the group's members.
- Run for a board position. This may increase your visibility in the community and raise the profile of your concern.
- Ask if your issue can be placed on the group's agenda.
- Consider whether joining with the group will move your issue closer toward its goals.

The following example shows how individual parents benefited when they pursued partnerships with others in their community. In this case, reaching out and finding others with shared experiences helped accelerate the benefits that can stem from the advocacy process.

Reaching Out to Find New Partners

In one community, there were a number of children with a variety of special needs. One child was hearing-impaired, another suffered from severe vision impairment, and others were delayed in their development and motor skills. Individually, the parents had not made any progress in having their children's needs met within the local elementary school. However, once the parents reached out to each other and combined forces, their actions met with greater success. As a group, advocating for all the community's children with special needs, they were able to have a greater impact than they would have as individual parents of a child with a disability. Ultimately, a revised curriculum was developed within the local school that addressed the special needs of this group of children.

What If No Group Exists?
Sometimes, even after carefully classifying your issue, using your community research tools, and pursuing your community resources, you might find that no group exists that can address your issue. That may be because your area does not offer a service, your problem is somewhat unique, or you are trailblazing a new path. If you cannot find an existing group to address your situation, Chapters IV and V will provide information and guidance on the steps needed to form your own action group.

CHAPTER IV: FORMING ACTION GROUPS

We must be the change we wish to see in the world.

Mohandas Ghandi (Indian leader)

There are as many reasons that people form groups as there are causes they address. This chapter is written in the spirit of the words expressed by Gandhi. It is designed to assist those who agree that, "We must be the change we wish to see in the world." Admittedly, there is no single route to advocacy that takes into account all the different paths and roadblocks advocates encounter. However, the directions in this chapter are intended to help any advocate form an action group. Read

together, Chapters III, IV, and V will provide practical advice on how to form your own action group. Whether an action group addresses issues of young children or older adolescents, or focuses on improving schools or neighborhoods, a successful group follows similar steps. A basic outline for forming your own action group includes:

✧ Step 1: Recruit others to join your effort
✧ Step 2: Arrange and conduct successful meetings
✧ Step 3: Select leaders

✛ Step 4: Determine appropriate action strategies
✛ Step 5: Make and implement a plan of action
✛ Step 6: Use public awareness strategies to advance your message

This chapter will discuss the first three steps in forming an action group. Chapter V will review the last three steps. Together, these six steps are guidelines for new entrants into the world of action groups and more seasoned readers. It is hoped that they both may gain further insight into the "how's" and "why's" of effective action. After describing these steps, this manual will take up a brief discussion of the importance of maintaining action groups. In dynamic and democratic societies, building action groups is important. However, maintaining them is also critical. Just as parents perform routine maintenance on their homes, action groups must also spend time maintaining their organizations and sustaining the enthusiasm of their members.

Step 1: Recruit Others to Join Your Effort
The first step in forming an action group is to get other people to join your effort. At this stage, you have likely pinpointed a community need, determined that it is not a "go-it-alone" issue, and are planning to form a group. The next questions are:

• Who else is affected by the issue?
• Who else might be affected?

To arrive at the answers, remember that users and potential users are all part of the pool of people you might want to consider as you seek to enlist the support of others.

Enlisting Support for Full-Day Kindergarten

One community was trying to get a full-day kindergarten program in their local school. For many years, there had only been a half-day program, which did not meet the needs of the community where both parents often worked full-time. To approach the question of "How do we get others to join?" parents contacted the current class, but also canvassed their neighborhood in search of "future users" of the program. They found there were many families in the neighborhood with young children who would be entering kindergarten in the following year. From this search of "current users" and "potential users" they were able to get many families to join their group. Ultimately, they were able to change the system to include a full-time kindergarten program for children in cases where both parents worked.

While this is just one example, the basic question remains, "How do you get others to join your effort?" Sometimes an effective means of recruiting support on an issue is to look close to home. Go door to door, call friends on the phone, or even stop acquaintances in the street to rally support. Be specific about what you need from them and be prepared to answer their questions such as:

- What is the situation?
- What do you want to accomplish?
- How do you plan to achieve this goal?
- How can I help?

Other ways to recruit helpers include:

- Make phone calls
- Write letters
- Distribute flyers
- Consider asking local businesses to help

When you talk to friends, distribute flyers, write letters, or make phone calls, make sure your message is succinct. A letter informing a community of an issue should be brief and to the point. A flyer, similarly, should clearly convey the issue and, more importantly, provide a way to get in touch with a group's organizers. Sometimes, an eye-catching paper color or interesting design can help get people's attention.

In one brochure for a children's advocacy group, the cover picture of a little red wagon was a quick visual aid to alert the reader to the fact the organization's purpose was to help children. The cover quote reiterated this theme with a caption by a prominent individual (General Colin Powell, U.S.A. (Ret.), Chairman of America's Promise) that played off this strong symbol of childhood. His words supported the graphics when he said, "The little red wagon. A symbol of childhood. It could be filled with a child's hopes and dreams or weighted down with their burdens. Millions of children need our help to pull that wagon along. Let's all pull together." This message, clearly conveyed in words and pictures, helped drive home the point that children were at the heart of this group's goals.

> Asking people face-to-face to join your group is the most effective way to rally support. Studies show that people are more likely to help when asked personally rather than when they are in a group situation.

In another example, a child's drawing of a flower in the sunshine was a heartwarming way to ask a community to pitch in and help clean up a park and plant flowers. The flyer was brief and friendly, with an upbeat tone like, "Join us as we clean up our park. Refreshments served. Fun for all!" Key information such as the date of clean-up, the time of the gathering, and a way to contact the organizer were all included. The flyer also suggested that people bring gloves to protect their fingers from broken glass and thorny plants in the park.

In the movie *Field of Dreams*, an enthusiastic baseball fan builds a dream baseball field in a remote cornfield. While many are doubtful, the man is convinced that others will come and join in the sport. In fact, his dream comes true, as other baseball enthusiasts fill the once overgrown cornfield to capacity. Unlike the movie, however, getting others to join in is not a magical event. It requires hard work, determination, and following a few basic steps, such as considering the useful role that simple group gatherings can play. You might want to hold a community dinner or a small block party in your neighborhood. The following shows how productive and fun a neighborhood function can be.

Picnics and Parties

In one community, the neighborhood had changed over time from primarily older citizens without children to families with young children. However, few seemed to know each other because they worked long hours and if they were at home, they were inside, caring for young children. One family took the initiative to hold a block party. A time and date were set on a weekend, when most families were home,  flyers were distributed in mailboxes, and families were encouraged to bring their favorite dishes. Because the neighborhood was multi-ethnic, the variety of foods was a way to open communication between people who had not previously had the opportunity or inclination to speak to each other. Adults organized children's games, from a "limbo contest" to a treasure hunt, with small candies as the reward. During the party, one family circulated petitions calling for street lights to be erected in the neighborhood. Many neighbors were not aware of the fact that the county required a certain number of signatures to grant street lights. All who were present signed and the volume of signatures played a persuasive role in getting street lights in the community. Parents, many of whom worked night shifts, felt much safer returning after work to a well-lit neighborhood. The successful picnic dinner became an annual neighborhood event that was eagerly anticipated by children and adults alike.

Recruiting people to join your action group is an important step. Another important component of any action group is knowing how to arrange and conduct effective meetings. The next section suggests a few ways to make meetings fun and productive.

Step 2: Arrange and Conduct Successful Meetings

Meetings are useful vehicles to bring together people and focus attention on issues. However, it is important that these meetings be productive or else people will not continue to come to them. The quickest way to learn what makes for a productive meeting is to consider what makes for an *unproductive* one:

- No clear agenda
- No time limit
- A loss of focus and leadership
- A sense that "nothing was accomplished"
- The meeting went "on and on," and people asked "what was the point?" when it was over

How do you avoid these common pitfalls? At a time when more and more meetings take place, from breakfast meetings to lunch meetings, formal and informal, what are the ingredients of a successful and productive meeting? While there are certain ingredients common to a good meeting, no two are alike. Some issues will require lengthy discussions and significant debate. Others may require less planning. However, whether the issue is simple or complex, common ingredients for effective meetings include:

- Advance preparation
- A clear agenda
- A clear time limit

Advance preparation for a productive meeting. Once you have arranged for others to join with you, the next step is to determine:

- Who will be invited?
- What is the focus of the meeting?
- When and where will the meeting be held?
- How are notices distributed?
- What items will be placed on an agenda?

Advance preparations are key to a well-run meeting. Anticipate issues that will arise, such as "Do we have enough seating and will there be child-care for night meetings?" Make sure the meeting is well advertised and organized and people know when and where it will be held. Some advance notice (one or two weeks time) is usually sufficient. However, too much advance notice (four to six weeks) can be detrimental and people may forget to come. Contact people ahead of time to remind them of the meeting and confirm the number of participants. Small meetings (which are often effective) can sometimes be held in each other's homes. If space is a problem, look for other locations. Contact organizations in your community that hold meetings on a regular basis. Ask religious institutions, businesses, and schools about using their space to hold your meeting and then, make a checklist to help the meeting run smoothly. Ask:

- Are there enough chairs and places to sit so all feel welcome?
- What time will the meeting be held?
- Will any food be served?

If this is a meeting for parents of small children, see if a room could be set aside for informal child care so parents can participate but don't have to go to the expense or burden of finding baby-sitters. Food and refreshments, which often generate conversation and allow people to mingle, can help reduce the anxiety of meeting people.

Prepare an agenda. Another ingredient for a productive meeting is an agenda prepared ahead of time. List the main issue as well as other related issues. Some people may not be able to stay for the whole time, and an agenda, either written on a large piece of paper or chalkboard that can be seen by all, lets participants know what will be discussed and who they can contact for more information. Provide extra pens, pencils, and paper for participants, some of whom might forget these items as they rush from work or caring for their child. Circulate a sign-in sheet that asks for participants' names and addresses, as well as a space for them to list how they can help. Provide a few suggestions (such as, note-taker, photographer, hostess), but also leave space for people to write down how they would like to assist. This list will be very helpful when it comes time to assigning tasks. Be sure to leave some time in your agenda for participants to ask questions. It is then that organizers will get a sense of the groups' interests and those who attend will not just feel like an "audience" of listeners, but will take on a more active role as participants in the process.

Learn about each other. Another objective for a meeting is to take time to learn who is interested in an issue and to make people feel comfortable with each other. One easy way to do this is through introductions. In a small group, introductions can easily be done. There are even a few ways to make this routine task more fun. Too often, people get used to standard ways to introduce people and tend not to pay attention during introductions. But, getting to know each other in a group is critical to a group's cohesion and its ability to act effectively. One way to help people listen is to ask a member to introduce the individual sitting next to him. Give the group a few minutes to talk to their partner and learn their name and a few details about their hobbies, interests, and family life. After their brief conversation, let them introduce each other to the group. This is one way members can learn about each other and build community at the same time.

Have a time limit. Everyone can probably recall a meeting that has gone on too long. In fact, even with a good cause, some groups have disintegrated because of unproductive use of time. Be considerate. Parents are busy people with multiple responsibilities. Sometimes evening meetings are the only times available, but even if there is child care, they can also present a burden on busy parents. Efficient meetings are a good way to ensure continued participation and encourage others to join. Word spreads that the group respects parents and uses its time well. One problem that can arise is that people often disagree on how best to address an issue. This, at times, can lead to lengthy debate. While debate is a healthy feature of democratic decision-making, excessive debate can become a problem. Place a time limit on the meeting as a whole (perhaps one hour) as well as a limit on individual debates, or for time-consuming issues, create a task force to recommend a course of action.

Make a follow-up plan to the meeting. One cardinal rule of meetings is, "Don't leave a meeting without setting up a time for the next meeting." If the participants leave before the next meeting time is determined, a lot of time will be wasted in contacting each and every participant again. Use the current meeting forum to establish the time, date, and location for a follow-up meeting, as well as to decide what unfinished business will be tackled at the next meeting. This can save a lot of time and effort on the part of organizers.

Step 3: Selecting Leaders
The third step in the journey to forming an effective group is to select strong leaders. Surprisingly, the qualifications for the "job" may be different from what many expect.

What are leadership qualities? In study after study, when a group of people is asked, "What makes good leaders?" the first words used to describe leaders are people who are "efficient," "do-it-aloners," individuals who are "outspoken," and can "take charge." However, when effective leadership styles are closely analyzed, it becomes clear that leadership calls for far different skills. In parent action groups, there are many leadership positions that need to be filled, from leading meetings to organizing fundraising activities, to heading up public education efforts. In all these areas, strong and productive leaders enable concerns to be translated into actions. When selecting leaders, look for people who can:

- Work well with others
- Delegate tasks
- Engender community respect
- Maintain calm and be level-headed
- Listen
- Share responsibility.
- Communicate effectively

Selecting leaders who can mobilize others is more important than recruiting do-it-aloners with an "island mentality." Without a group, there is no one to lead. One need only look to the sky to notice that a flock of geese, without a leader, can stray off course and a lead goose, without its followers, is simply flying alone. Likewise, those who are so efficient and capable as not to need the support of others can alienate the very groups they need for support. As the following example indicates, sometimes a leader who is "outspoken" may turn out to be "hot-headed" and unable to clearly and calmly articulate a groups' needs.

Leaders Should Be Team Players

In a community of busy, working families, one leader enthusiastically chosen by the school PTO (Parent Teacher Organization) at first seemed like the ideal choice. She had, single-handedly, beautified the school grounds by planting a garden by herself. When she noticed how busy other parents were, she continued to maintain the garden, weed it, and even plant seasonal flowers all for the enjoyment of others and without any other "helping hands." However, as time went on, it became clear that this "leader," was a "do-it-aloner" who failed to rally critical team support. Although she thought she was helping the group by not bothering them with details (distributing flyers, setting up meetings), this "island mentality" was in fact harmful to group cohesion. The inability to delegate tasks led to a significant decline in parent involvement and ultimately a loss of group momentum. Moreover, in an important meeting with the school principal, the leader became so impassioned that the dynamic of the meeting turned hostile. Finally, it became clear that the qualities of good leadership required a "team player," a "level-headed" person, and one who was known and respected within the community.

THE TEN QUALITIES OF EFFECTIVE LEADERSHIP

The following checklist is provided to help advocates choose good leaders. A good leader should:

1. *BE ABLE TO IDENTIFY A MISSION THAT MATTERS.* Have the ability to identify missions that matter and have a chance for successful outcomes.
2. *BE COMMITTED.* A special amount of dedication and commitment to a cause are key.
3. *BE ETHICAL AND USE POWER WISELY.* Leadership entails power. Those who fairly and ethically exercise this power are likely to maintain community respect. This is important so others will listen to the message and the community will want to be involved.
4. *BE WILLING TO SEEK CHANGE.* Advocacy involves change. Good leaders are not reluctant to stir up "the system."
5. *BE A RISK TAKER.* Leadership involves risks. There are no guarantees when trying to effect change. Good leaders are not put off by setbacks, but have the ability to take risks, rally, reassess, and try again.
6. *BE A DECISION-MAKER.* A good leader will be able to move a diverse group toward consensus with fair decision-making abilities and a healthy dose of compromise.
7. *BE AN EFFECTIVE COMMUNICATOR.* A group's aims are not effective unless they are well communicated to key decision-makers. A good leader is also a good communicator. Effective speaking plays an important role in defining a good leader.
8. *BE A GOOD LISTENER.* Good listening skills make up an equally important part. The ability to hear others, synthesize their viewpoints, and even respond appropriately to opposing views is key.
9. *BE A TALENT SCOUT.* Be able to uncover hidden talents in your community. Seek out committed, dedicated individuals. Find the support of artists, business people, parents, and others.
10. *BE A TEAM BUILDER.* A strong group is one that has diverse talents, resources, and viewpoints from which a leader can draw. Reaching out to other parents is an important skill. Enlist and include others with diverse backgrounds and experiences. This makes for a strong team.

CHAPTER V: USING ACTION GROUPS TO TAKE ACTION

Opportunities multiply as they are seized.

Sun Tzu (Ancient Chinese Scholar)

This chapter continues to lay the groundwork for action by providing additional directions for advocacy. Taking time at the outset to organize and prepare effectively will pay off in the long run. At this stage, you have already done much of the hard work, from gathering facts, recruiting others to join your group, holding successful meetings and delegating responsibilities. With your issue clearly defined and the support of others in your community, your action group is now ready to make a difference. As you or your group get poised to take action, it is important to focus on the final steps to complete your advocacy journey. These steps are briefly described in this chapter and include:

✢ Step 4: Determine appropriate strategies
✢ Step 5: Make a plan of action
✢ Step 6: Use public awareness strategies to advance your message

Step 4: Determine Appropriate Strategies

All action groups need to determine appropriate strategies to advance their group's goals. Fortunately, parents who become advocates are often well prepared for this task. Raising children requires parents to constantly exercise their ability to match strategies to situations. When children fall on the playground, parents decide whether to comfort them with calming words, apply a bandage, or if the fall is serious, take them to a doctor or the hospital. Similarly, working in an  action group requires the use of these same decision-making skills in determining appropriate strategies. The difference is that the decisions are no longer whether to apply a bandage or take a trip to the doctor. Rather, the question is how to match your group's goals to an appropriate strategy that will increase the likelihood of a successful outcome.

Action group strategies vary depending on the issue. They can range from deciding whom to approach on a school-related issue (a teacher, principal, or school board), to deciding whether group or one-on-one meetings with parents would be most effective. Strategies include considering whether your group will be most effective working on its own, joining a larger, more established group, or even partnering with a local business to help move your issue ahead. As you develop strategies for action, recall that when you began this journey you asked several questions such as, "Am I the only one with this concern?" and "Is this an appropriate issue?" As you progress along the journey, questions continue to play an important role in determining strategies. This chapter provides several general questions that are designed to help determine an appropriate strategy and shape a plan of action. When you feel confident in your ability to answer most of the following questions, then it will be time to make your own plan of action.

- Can you describe your issue clearly to others?
- Is your organizational structure in place? (Do you have members, leaders, etc.?)
- Do you know your allies and your opponents?
- Are you aware of key decision-makers? (Is it a principal? A neighborhood association?)
- Do you know where to go for support? (For information? To recruit new members?)
- Are you ready to make convincing presentations? (Informally, to friends? Formally, at meetings?)

Much in the way you decided at the beginning to go it alone or join a group, a group also engages in the same process of deciding whether to go it alone or partner with a larger organization. Another related set of questions on this subject is whether to address your issue through:

- Regular channels (work within your own group)
- Coalition-building strategies (join with another group or look for more partners)

There are pluses and minuses to each approach. The first example shows how one group decided that it was an appropriate strategy to maintain their independence from other organizations. The next two examples show the benefits of reaching out to other community organizations to further a group's goals.

The Benefits of Autonomy

Sometimes, a group may have greater autonomy and decision-making ability when working alone. This was the case in a local school where the PTO (Parent Teacher Organization), a school-based group, needed to decide whether or not to join the PTA (Parent Teacher Association), a national organization. In the case of the particular school, the community voted to remain separate. After much discussion, the parents felt  they would lose some of their autonomy if they joined the national group, because they would have to adopt the agenda of a national organization with which they did not always agree. On their own, even if some of their resources would remain smaller, overall, the independence to make their own decisions, without consulting another larger structure, proved the winning argument.

However, there are times when joining with a larger organization will add name recognition that can propel an issue to the forefront and also make the resources of a more established organization available to a smaller group. What follows are two situations in which a community partnership strategy (coalition-building) proved beneficial to action groups.

The Benefits of Community Partnerships

Sometimes, businesses can be useful partners to action groups. In one community, local businesses played an important role in increasing the involvement of children in sports. Parents asked small businesses, such as restaurants and grocery stores, to sponsor teams. In return, the stores had their names printed on the children's T-shirts. Photographs of the store owners with the teams were taken and posted in the local stores. When the local paper covered the children's games, the stores received free publicity for their community service. Parents took notice of stores they had not previously visited. Children, who had lacked basic sports equipment, were now able to have enough balls for soccer practice from the local businesses. The whole community benefited.

In another community, many parents worked with a local video store to reinforce community values and help children work harder in school. Some parents objected to the disparity between the number of violent films available to their children compared to a lack of educational videos and parenting tapes. A few parents contacted the local video store as a resource and encouraged the store to provide rewards (free rentals) to children who earned good grades on their report cards. They posted large signs in their storefronts announcing that free videos would be given to children with a high number of A's and B's on their report cards. This incentive motivated the children to work harder and a new partnership was formed. Ultimately, the store became a community resource tied into the values families wanted to instill in their children, striving to earn good grades in school. The store was also able to purchase more educational tapes for children and move them closer to the entrance, while moving the more violent films the community had objected to farther back in the store. The store's business grew and the parents were also rewarded with a better selection of videos for their children.

Step 5: Make a Plan of Action

Asking questions is one way to help a group develop a successful plan of action. In Step 4, as you determined appropriate strategies, you posed several questions to make sure your group was ready to take action. With those questions answered, the next and most important step is to make a plan of action. In this section, there are series of action questions that build on the earlier strategy questions and should be part of any action plan.

This section also provides a sample action plan chart. It is based on an example of how one community tried to improve the nutritional value of lunches in an elementary school. This example, and more importantly, the steps that were taken, are clearly charted to guide groups through the process of designing their own plan of action.

While every group tackles its own set of unique questions and issues as it develops an action plan, all groups share some common elements. They share a need to build a group, determine appropriate strategies, and develop a clear plan of action. A checklist of questions, like those that follow, can be a useful device to make sure you are well prepared for the journey. Although you will want to tailor this list to fit your situation, these questions can be a starting point.

Action Questions:
- What goals do you want to achieve? In the short term? In the long term?
- Who is the target audience for your actions?
- What are your resources?
- What preparation steps are necessary to reach your goal(s)?
- What action steps are necessary?
- What group positions do you need to fill (treasurer, secretary, etc.)?
- What is your timeline for action?
- How will you evaluate the impact of your work?

SAMPLE ACTION PLAN CHART:
ISSUE: IMPROVING NUTRITION IN SCHOOL LUNCHES

Goals	Target Audience	Action Steps	Timeline	Who's Responsible?	Evaluation
• <u>Get more nutritious lunches served at school</u>	School principal or other administrators	1. Gather information about issue	1st week	(fill in name or names for each action step)	<u>Evaluate short-term goals:</u>
1a. Short-term: Educate children and teachers/administrator, if necessary, about benefits of nutrition to children's growth and development.	Parent association School dietician or school nurse	2. Recruit support from other concerned parents 3. Determine if other groups are working on issue and whether to join forces	2nd week 2nd week		Were children educated on the importance of nutritious meals? Teachers? Can you quantify any of your successes?
1b. Long-term: Replace "junk" food or empty calories with more nutritious choices at lunch	Teachers Children	4. Assign responsibilities 5. Conduct meetings with parent group	3rd week 3rd week		What have you learned about the effectiveness of your strategies? <u>Evaluate long-term goals:</u>
		6. Make presentation to principal and/or other administrators about concern and importance of nutritious lunch	4th week		Did nutritious food replace "junk" food?
Integrate nutrition into the school curriculum		7. Conduct public awareness activities (e.g., make posters for school, include information in school newsletter)	5th week		Did teachers integrate the topic of nutrition into the curriculum?
		8. Work with teachers to bring in nutrition information	5th week		Can you measure or quantify any of your successes? What have you learned about the effectiveness of your strategies?

61

When you review your own issue for action, consider how you would fill in the information in each column of the action plan. Do you know your target audience? Can you distinguish your long-term goals from your more immediate goals? Have you delegated tasks to others? Is someone responsible for planning the meetings? Is there someone else who can be a spokesperson? Have you done the preparation necessary to take action (gathered facts, assessed community needs)? Do you know how much time and effort your action steps will take? Are you ready to take action to make a difference?

Obviously, communities face multiple and different needs. Many newly formed or first-time advocacy groups prefer to choose as their starting point simple, easily obtainable goals, and, later, progress to more complex goals. Beginning with issues that are more easily addressed provides people with time and experience to develop skills needed to address greater challenges. It also generates enthusiasm from early successes that can be used to keep members involved and attract new members to a cause. With some of these issues in mind, it is time to move ahead and chart your own plan of action.

As you review the questions on your own or in a group, be honest in your assessment. The more time you take to consider the steps in an action plan, the more time you have to address them. For instance, a group that has a clear understanding of the time factors relating to their issues will make sure to report on assignments by a given time and act in the allotted time frame. Likewise, a group that knows its target audience and key decision-maker will have time to canvas a community for contacts and prepare current members to articulate the case before a group. As you fill out your own action chart, keep in mind some of the tasks that are common to all groups. In addition to issues already discussed, for an action plan to be most effective, you will need to do the following.

Assign responsibilities. A well-run action group involves many roles and responsibilities. Some of the positions that need to be filled in many action groups include secretary (note-taker at meetings), vice-president (co-leader), public relations person (spreads the word about the group), host (organizes refreshments), and fund-raiser (helps plan bake sales, approaches local businesses about donating merchandise or money to a good cause). The previous action plan chart describes some of the action steps that one group seeking more nutritious lunches in an elementary school needed to assign. In general, if members of a group have spent time learning about each other, the group will be more likely to make use of individuals' talents because it has uncovered them. As you complete the section on responsibilities, consider the needs of your group as well as its resources.

Evaluate resources. As you make your plan of action, try to make use of everyone's talents. In the case of the plan to have better lunches at school, a group that has an involved parent with a background in nutrition, nursing, or health, may be able to make a more convincing case. Also, let people try different jobs. Sometimes an organization benefits by having people take a break from their regular assignments. Let the secretary try her hand at writing up an information sheet about an issue, or let the treasurer organize a fundraising event. Developing new talent is not only beneficial to the group, but a good way to develop personal skills that will help in parenting, job-hunting, and even in relationships. Building a community action organization is not a separate experience from building other community relations. The skills developed in a group experience are useful in many ways as the following example illustrates.

Puppet Show on Inclusive Education

When one group found out that its member was a puppeteer, the woman performer put her skills to use in writing and performing a puppet show in town. This was a new and fun way to rally support for the cause of helping children with disabilities gain access to a regular classroom. It also was educational in that the use of puppets in the performance was a non-threatening way to illustrate the problems faced by children who were excluded from participating in class activities.

Develop timelines to match your short- and long-term goals. We all depend on timelines in our daily life, from when to pay bills to how much time we give our children to brush their teeth, pack their books, and leave for school. Timelines help keep individuals and groups on track. That is why it is important for an action group to ask, "What do we want to accomplish and by when?" Clear goals and fixed dates for action are also important to action groups. As you develop an agenda, the organizers of a group need to set time limits for each meeting, but also need to specify clear-cut goals for each task. While groups require some flexibility, in general fixed dates for meetings, clear-cut goals, both short- and long-term, help the overall effectiveness of a plan. For instance, a combination of short-term goals (improved education on nutrition) and long-term goals (improving the quality of the food served at lunch) are both important. Working in accordance with a school calendar and meeting with school officials when school is in session, rather than over the summer (when key decision-makers may not be available) is one benefit of using a timeline in planning.

Document your work. Clearly documenting your work is an essential part of the process of advocacy. This is important for many reasons. First, it helps make people accountable because written records are a form of public acknowledgement of tasks, requests, and actions. Secondly, recording your plans and action steps will provide useful data for present and future members of your group. For example, noting that, "I called the Mayor's office three days before the accident and requested that the traffic light be fixed," is important and useful information. This type of documentation of your work lends credibility and a professional tone to your efforts.

Evaluate your work. An important question for all groups is to develop ways to assess their work. Reviewing what has been done, and what still needs to be accomplished, will help in future efforts. Sometimes, there are objective measures to evaluate progress. When parents are asked how their children are doing, they may be asked questions like, "Are they growing? Are they gaining weight? Do they have many friends? Are they doing well in school?" However, more often than not in parenting, evaluating a child's development is not a matter of objective measurements. Similarly, evaluating a group's objectives is a combination of different criteria.

In the case of the group that sought more nutritious lunches in school, one way to evaluate success would be to compare the nutritional value of the meals before the group took action and after the group's efforts. However, there are also other less objective criteria that are equally important in measuring success. Perhaps the group fell short of significantly altering the lunchroom choices. Nevertheless, they were able to educate students on the importance of nutrition, involve the school nurse in helping teachers plan curriculum for a "health day," and inform parents about healthy eating that carried over into children's breakfast and dinner choices at home. These measures of "success" are just as important.

Step 6: Using Public Awareness Strategies to Advance the Message

Determining appropriate strategies and making a plan of action are critical to any action group. However, alone, these steps are not sufficient. An informed community is better equipped to understand how an issue affects the lives of its members and more likely to do something to address the needs of the community. A clear and well-presented message can enhance the likelihood of a cause's success. Using public awareness to advance the message about a situation can serve to teach a community about its needs. Gaining support for an issue can be just the push a cause needs to turn intentions into actions. While there is a wide disparity in access to communication tools around the world, from countries where citizens rely on word of mouth, to those who have access to the Internet, the similarities in using public awareness to advance a message outweigh the differences. No matter how the message is presented, a well-organized use of a community's publicity resources can:

- Increase public awareness of and support for an issue
- Educate the public and enhance the visibility of an issue
- Spark dialogue
- Build constituencies

When people are aware of an issue, it helps them develop a sense of urgency about the problem and feel, like you, that "something needs to be done." It also can help forge a group's public identity and even enlarge a group's membership. Ultimately, this can help motivate bureaucracies and decision-makers to change. It can also help:

- Define the problem
- Target an appropriate audience
- Focus public attention
- Present proposals for a solution
- Provide contact information
- Solicit resources to solve a problem

This section will provide steps that groups can take to make the most of their efforts to inform the public of the worthiness of their cause.

Monitor the media and other public awareness efforts. Do your "media" homework. Which of your community papers carry issues of local interest? Who are the reporters that cover "human interest" stories? Develop contacts and ask your friends whom they know. It may be that someone in your group already has a good relationship with a local reporter. Your group may want to create a media list of journalists, newspapers, radio shows, and others who report on school and neighborhood issues. When your group has its issue defined and is ready to meet with the press or even publish its own newsletter, choose those journalists and sources identified as having expressed an interest in community events.

Prepare written material (press releases). Sometimes an effective piece of written material can help further a group's aims. Press releases are short, catchy written descriptions that provide factual information about a group, such as "What is the issue of concern?" "What can be done about the situation?" and "Who is available to discuss the situation further?" An event, no matter how clever, is only as valuable as the worthiness of the cause and the enthusiasm it inspires. If a group  decides to orchestrate a publicity event (for example, to have children perform songs in public to draw attention to the need for music education in school), it must also take several steps in advance, including providing information on "When" the event takes place and "Where" it will be held.

Written material explaining a group's aims (a press release), can be delivered to local papers in advance to give organizations time to assign reporters to cover an event. Follow-up contact a day or two ahead of time helps remind the reporters of an upcoming event. Similar steps should be taken if a group decides to call a press conference. Other ways to gain support and attention include writing to editors of major newspapers, including a contact person's name with a story suggestion. Whatever methods an advocacy group chooses to enhance its visibility in the community, the most important points to keep in mind are that the information should be:

- Accurate
- Factual
- Concise
- Up-to-date
- Informative (include contact person's name, number)
- Presented in an attractive manner (children's drawings can be very effective)

Match communication strategies to your audience. Public awareness campaigns should take into account the fact that members of a community may be diverse, speak different languages, and observe distinct traditions. Material in different languages, such as bilingual signs and newsletters, are all ways to reach out to different segments of society. In one school, every room, from the bathrooms to the lunchroom had a sign on the door written in five different languages to help children in a diverse community find their way around
the school. Ensuring that meetings and rallies are not scheduled on culturally significant days further shows an awareness of cultural differences.

Religious Awareness

In one school district, the first day of school often coincided with a religious group's most important celebration. This often got the school year off to a bitter start as parents had to choose between having their children observe their religious tradition at home and integrating them into their school and community. It turned out that the administration was unaware of the conflict until the group's religious leader wrote a letter to the local paper. This public awareness strategy, of using the local paper to increase community awareness, helped resolve an ongoing problem that had in part been prolonged by a lack of public knowledge of the issue.

Use visual aids. The saying, "A picture is worth a thousand words" underscores how visual aids (photographs, catchy posters, homemade signs) can advance an issue. The media is a potent vehicle because it quickly distributes a message to many. What is likely to get a reporter's attention is also likely to be attention getting to readers. Posters made by children have a way of touching the public unlike that of adult-made banners or signs. One children's organization that sought improved medical services for children with disabilities used a colorful picture on a giant banner to indicate the severity of the need. This caught the attention of a local photographer and the story was circulated throughout the community. With

the community focused on the issue, a local hospital sent assistance. Parent "assistants" were trained by hospital staff to provide physical therapy to children at a local school.

Distribute information. Public campaigns need to reach the public. Newsletters, pamphlets, and brochures can be distributed to areas frequented by parents (providing there are no laws against this approach in your community). Public places, such as libraries, hospitals, schools and religious institutions, are often good places to distribute literature. However, in many communities there are strict regulations prohibiting the distribution of literature and posting of flyers in store fronts and bulletin boards. Community members should become informed about their local laws and regulations on this subject before distributing information.

Orchestrate an event. In some cases, heightening community interest in an issue is as simple as writing a "Letter to the Editor." In other cases, a larger effort must be undertaken to help a cause. At one local school, there was a shortage of musical instruments. To remedy this situation, a group of children and their music teacher borrowed instruments and performed a concert outside a local school official's budget meeting. The concert so moved the administrators that a way was found to save the school music program.

Interview tips. If your issue has gained widespread attention, it is likely that someone from your group will be interviewed. Select an individual who is a good speaker, well-respected, and informed on your issue as spokesperson. The group may wish to draw up some agreed-on issues to discuss before an interview. These should be key points the group would like the public to know about. Honest answers like, "I don't know" are preferable to responses like, "No comment." Sometimes, it may seem like journalists have made up their mind on the issue ahead of time. A good interviewee will redirect conversation when necessary and calmly state the group's aims and objectives. Other times, after the interview is in print, a group may feel that its viewpoint was misconveyed or there might even be factual errors. If the misstatement is so severe as to potentially harm the cause, call the journalist for a correction. Some groups use the "Letters to the Editor" column in the local newspaper as a way to restate their opinions and clarify any errors.

Clearly, there are many different kinds of public awareness strategies that can be used to widen the circle of information and prolong an issue's impact on a community. Whichever strategy your group pursues, the communication method should match the community and make use of its resources. Now that much of the hard work has been done, the next question that arises is simple yet important, "What do I do next?" Chapter VI will offer some guidance on how to answer this question and more importantly will discuss how to sustain a group's momentum, maintain a group's enthusiasm, celebrate your efforts, and have some fun.

CHAPTER VI: SUSTAINING MOMENTUM AND CELEBRATING SUCCESS

To leave the world a bit better, whether by a healthy child, a garden patch; to know even one life has breathed easier because you have lived. This is to have succeeded.

Ralph Waldo Emerson (American writer and philosopher)

At this point in the journey you have traveled quite some distance. Possibly as far as from someone who a short time ago only imagined "doing something" to someone who has taken action. So, now, the question arises, "What do I do next?" Whether your issue has been "won" or you still have a long way to travel to where you want to be, it is time to take a breather. Like travelers everywhere, it is important to take rest stops, stretch your legs, and refuel. But unlike a road trip, a rest stop in an advocacy journey is not the same as simply getting refreshments or taking an unexpected side-trip. Rather, it involves asking fundamental questions and taking time out to celebrate your efforts and have some fun.

How Do You Keep a Group Together?

On a road-trip, passengers stay together because they enjoy each other's company and rely on one another to arrive safely at their destination. Sometimes, they play games, sing songs, or stop for food to boost their energy and sustain their momentum for travel. Likewise, sustaining an action group's momentum means paying attention to many issues, from sustaining the organizational structure to maintaining the group's enthusiasm

for action. To do both requires efforts on several fronts, including ongoing communication with members, accurate record-keeping, and developing positive ways to praise members for their work. Attention to these and other organizational matters can help solidify a group's sense of purpose and partnership. When a group stays together, it can then move beyond "one-time fixes," and become an established part of a community, meeting new challenges as they appear. This section will take up the dual and related questions of how to:

✛ Sustain the organizational structure of a group
✛ Maintain enthusiasm among a group's members

Sustaining the Organizational Structure
Sustaining the organization you have developed can be a challenge. The following are suggestions for action groups to keep in mind.

Remain flexible. There are many ways that an organization can increase its chances of staying together. One way is for an action group to remain flexible, welcoming to new members, and open to new issues. Unlike action groups, bureaucracies are often embroiled in a web of routine. They maintain a rigid adherence to the status quo and are resistant to change. Parents who have encountered bureaucracies often report being told, "You must understand, there are certain procedures that must be followed before we can do anything for your child." Or they are subjected to excuses from bureaucrats who repeat phrases like, "It's not my fault. It's the system. I can't do anything about it." Successful action groups take a different approach. They tend to be flexible, adaptable, and responsive. Whereas a bureaucracy adheres to "standard operating procedures," action groups strive to seek new solutions when "old" responses fail. They try to do something about a situation, even if the system "never has."

Be prepared to grow. Often, achieving a group's aims is not the end of the mission, but the start of a new one. Whereas a group might set out on its journey with the initial objective of improving nutrition in the school, its mission can broaden in scope. The group may decide to tackle related issues and seek to integrate health education into the children's school curriculum. Or, they might reach out to the community and bring in local dentists and other health care providers who will instruct children on the importance of personal health care. Sometimes, as groups grow and their missions evolve, other structural changes take place. A growing group may need to deal with issues associated with a larger membership, finding meeting space to accommodate more people, and finding new ways to communicate with a growing membership.

Address legal issues. A host of legal and financial issues also emerge as action groups grow. For instance, a group may need to formally register as a non-governmental organization (NGO) to remain in compliance with local laws. This is a formal procedure whose rules and regulations vary by state, country, and region, each with its own set of requirements. While a discussion of the specific legal and financial regulations associated with registering as an NGO is outside the scope of this book, groups would be well advised to consult with their community's lawyers and legal associations to learn about the relevant laws and remain in compliance with their area's requirements and regulations.

Maintaining a Group's Integrity

It is important that the good intentions and good reputation of the group remain at the forefront of all its activities. Operating an action group that is successful over the long run requires some basic operational and administrative activities. The following are the most important to consider.

Accurate record-keeping. Keeping accurate records of what an organization has done (minutes of past meetings), who has been involved (membership lists), and who a group has contacted (leaders, media, decision-makers) is critical to sustaining a group. If new leaders take over a group, records of past projects, resources, and membership lists will help them pick up where others have left off and save time that would be wasted building an organization from the ground up.

Good record-keeping is also vital when it comes to the issue of accounting for a group's finances. Action groups need to be able to account for where money comes from (donations, collections, bake sales) and where it goes (refreshments, advertising, etc.). While a treasurer may play a significant role in recording financial matters, all the leaders of the group should pay attention to these financial issues. The ability of a group to accurately account for its finances, from fundraising through fairs, donations from businesses, bake sales, and other events reflects on the group's overall integrity. Action groups that fail to handle their money well risk hurting their reputation and ability to promote their cause and attract new members.

Fundraising Can be Fun

One community youth group had fun fundraising when it wanted to raise money for sports equipment and team uniforms. The teenagers decided to hold a car and bike wash to raise money for gas to get them to "away" games and replace tattered team uniforms and deflated soccer balls. They contacted a local gas station that agreed to let them  use their space and water hoses on a hot summer weekend. The students waved handmade signs directing traffic to their car wash and let the public know (by holding up sturdy signs) that the money would be for a good cause. The teenagers had fun, cooling off in the hot afternoon washing cars, the gas station enjoyed additional business as car owners stopped to gas up as they waited for the wash, and the organization raised enough money for the next season's equipment and uniform needs.

Evaluate the group's work. Another way to maintain a group's structural integrity is to develop a plan to evaluate its work. After undertaking an issue, it is important to take an objective look at the steps taken and the goals achieved. Just as travelers recall the highlights and low points of their trips, advocacy travelers should set aside a time to evaluate what they have accomplished. Ask, what have we achieved? What would we still like to accomplish? How could we have done something better, or differently? Just as we sit with our children and evaluate their school work, or receive job evaluations ourselves, evaluating an action group is an important step in the whole process. The more honest and forthcoming a group is in its own assessment, the greater the chance it has of eventually reaching its goals. Thoughtful evaluation, from talking with members to writing down a list of achievements, are all ways to help people learn from their experiences. After you and your group have performed a self-assessment, then it is time to celebrate the journey and take time to have some fun.

Maintaining Enthusiasm

Members are the heart and soul of any organization. Action groups, like democracies, thrive on the involvement of people who are their most important resource. The key ingredient to any successful action group is a willingness of members to speak out, engage in fact-finding, contact decision-makers, rally community support, and put their energy behind a good cause. Therefore, it is essential that groups nourish and encourage member's enthusiasm. Keeping a group together requires promoting a sound organizational structure, but more impor-
tantly, it requires promoting the continued interest of a group's current members and efforts aimed at attracting new members. Below are a few ways to sustain and promote members' enthusiasm and involvement.

Encourage communication. A healthy action group requires ongoing communication with current members. Depending on the size of a group, there are different approaches to communication. One effective way to maintain group cohesion is through an informal method of communication. This means keeping members and others in the community aware of developments by talking to them. In the early stages of action groups, there is often a lack of time or resources to print a newsletter on a topic of concern. If that is the case, informal information sharing in supermarkets, religious institutions, on the sidewalk, or wherever people gather is one way to "spread the word" about a group's activities.

Formal information sharing through newsletters, on a regular basis (weekly or monthly), is also an important way to maintain an action group. Formal communication can:

- Keep current members informed of group progress.
- Provide focus for a group by requiring the group to put its aims and needs in writing.
- Provide key information, such as names and numbers of current members.

Newsletters can help clarify the needs of a group by making sure the message is well-presented and that people are aware of how an issue affects their lives. For example, a newsletter, published in a language of a minority group is an effective tool in recruiting members from segments of the population that may have been excluded due to a language barrier. Organizations often use newsletters as a way to recruit new members. As a group grows and becomes more established, it may want to charge small membership fees. These fees can be used to cover mailing costs and pay for other ongoing expenses.

Continue recruiting members. A well-run action group requires continuous recruitment of new members to supplement the energy and enthusiasm of current members, and to replace departing members.

A group that becomes overly dependent on a few individuals runs the risk of disintegrating when people leave (due to health or job issues), relocate, or become involved in other issues. New people bring new ideas and talents. A group that becomes exclusive may miss opportunities to attract new talent. Healthy advocacy groups require sustaining interest among current members and attracting new members. Asking around in a community and announcing openings (photographers, writers, etc.) is a way to attract new members and tap into talents. Holding meetings and introducing new members by name can make people feel welcome. The following example shows how ongoing recruitment and flexibility helped a group maintain its cohesiveness and effectiveness.

Keeping Up With Change

One women's group had become very successful. It had organized to improve the community, mentoring young girls in school, helping disadvantaged neighbors collect shoes for children, and supporting many good causes. However, as time went on, attendance at meetings fell and the group no longer had the "women-power" to  accomplish its tasks. As some members asked around they came to understand the source of the problem. Conversations among former members revealed that over time, this group of energetic, young women, all about the same age, had in a large part become mothers. The "free time" that they once devoted to "causes" was now devoted to their family. Night meetings, when their young children were getting ready for bed, were no longer possible. The women were not comfortable trading time with their children for time with the group. As it became clear what the problem was, the group re-grouped, held meetings at more convenient hours, provided co-op childcare during meeting time, and broadened the membership to include new members of different ages and life-stages. Bringing in others re-energized the group. Once again, the group was able to focus and undertook a number of toy drives, food drives, and clothing exchanges that benefited the community.

Award efforts and recognize progress. Another important component in the process of keeping a group together is making sure to take time to award efforts and recognize progress, not just outcomes. Work without reward can become drudgery. As parents, we encourage our children in many ways. When they are young, we smile at them to show them our pleasure and find that the warmth of our expressions are often mirrored back in their faces. Teachers also find that encouragement reaps rewards in motivating students to learn. In school, some teachers grade children for effort as well as achievement. Adults share similar motivations. They enjoy a pat on the back, a word of thanks for trying, not only for achieving. The short amount of time it takes to say "Thank you" is well worth the rewards. Expressing positive feelings increases the likelihood that members will remain involved and even recruit their friends to join. A simple "Thank you," said in earnest to someone who has participated in a group activity, or presenting "awards" such as flowers can help a group in many ways. It can:

- Raise the morale of the group
- Raise the profile of a group in a community
- Encourage members to continue their work
- Encourage new members to join

Celebrate experiences. People enjoy celebrations. A child's birthday party, a student's graduation celebration, and a couple's wedding celebration are all ways in which a community of people comes together to take the time to recognize personal and professional accomplishments. Action groups also benefit from taking time to celebrate efforts. Honoring members for their involvement in action groups can boost a group's morale and its profile and attract additional community interest. Presenting awards (flowers, plaques, and certificates) to members and acknowledging their hard work is an important part of keeping a group together. Gatherings that celebrate the action group's progress can help keep members motivated and increase the personal satisfaction that comes from working for a good cause and toward a common goal.

Celebrations Signal Satisfaction

In a large school, one parents' group had accomplished many improvements in its first year of activity. Parent "helpers" fixed fences that had been falling down, put down mulch in the school vegetable garden, and helped hang student art in the hallways. Even the children had participated in beautifying school grounds and planting a school flower and vegetable garden. The "Cucumber Kids" had such a successful crop that they were able to  barter with local merchants for basic school supplies, such as paper and pencils in the classroom. At the end of the year, a celebration was planned to honor those who had given so much of their time and enthusiasm to benefiting the school. Flowers, grown in the school garden, were presented to the parents. Concrete garden stepping stones with the imprint of the helping children's hands were made with the help of a parent and retired stonemason. The stones were placed in the school's outdoor garden as a symbol of gratitude. An awards ceremony held to honor those who played a role in the projects was well attended. The following year, many previously uninvolved parents became involved as a result of the community enthusiasm generated at a simple awards ceremony.

As all journeys near completion, travelers often ask, "Did I take the best route?" "Would I travel with those friends again?" Would I choose a different destination?" Similarly, as advocacy journey nears its destination, it is also time for review and introspection. Assessing a group's successes as well as its shortcomings can better prepare travelers for future trips. A good trip is filled with fun memories, a desire for further travel, and even lessons learned about how to make the next trip better. For an advocacy journey to be a fulfilling process, it is important not only to consider the details, from fact-gathering to list-making, but also to develop ways to celebrate the trip.

Organizing a group and putting forward new goals is a community-building experience. But, viewed on another level, it is more about meeting people, making friends, learning new skills that can make one a better parent, a stronger person, and a more capable citizen. It also involves applying newfound skills to situations that arise in every community as people strive to take action. What follows in the next and final chapter are a number of individual stories of advocacy. Around the world, in every community, there are countless examples of people who have made a difference. Chapter VII chooses a few moving examples from this richly diverse tapestry of people who identified a need and took action to improve their communities.

CHAPTER VII: REAL-LIFE EXAMPLES OF ADVOCATES IN ACTION

The best way to predict the future is to invent it.

Alan Kay (Apple Computers)

This chapter presents more detailed examples of real-life situations where people took action to improve their communities. The examples are based on people around the world, from teachers in Slovakia to artists in the United States, from classroom situations to neighborhood needs. Although no one manual can touch upon the myriad situations that families encounter every day, there are enough common threads that run through every community to suggest that these examples can help provide some useful tools to motivate others to work toward common goals.

Even if the details of the situations differ from one's own experiences, simply knowing that there are many ways to seek change can be inspiring and motivating. The lessons vary, but what remains constant is that all the advocates in action are people who turned a need into an opportunity to make a difference. Using their advocacy tools, they turned "stumbling blocks" into "stepping stones." Future advocates who read these stories will hopefully use these experiences to inspire them to make a difference in their communities.

GRANDPARENTS BUILD BETTER FUTURES FOR CHILDREN

Grandparents around the world play an important role in building a better future for children and their community. While many possess life-long skills as retired farmers, teachers, carpenters and doctors, more importantly, their strong connection and love for children motivates them to become involved. Below are a few ways that grandparents have used their love of children and talents acquired over a lifetime to benefit their communities.

In Kazakhstan, a "Grandmothers' Club" organized a weaving project with a group of children in a local school. The children were taught to weave, prepare wool, and make their own rugs. At the end of the lesson, the classroom had many beautiful rugs made by grandmothers and children working together. The grandmothers then organized a sale in which some of the rugs were sold in the community to purchase boots for children who had been unable to attend class in the winter because they lacked proper footwear. The remaining rugs were used in the classroom and served the practical purpose of making the room warmer and quieter. More importantly, they were a wonderful reminder of the strong ties between the two generations.

In Kyrgyzstan, a retired grandmother who was a doctor used her skills to improve the educational curriculum at a local school. She came into school twice a month and conducted a workshop on the subject of healthy lifestyles, proper nutrition, and the importance of good dental care. Although the school lacked sufficient staff to assist children with disabilities, this grandmother used her professional skills to assist these children. She provided massages to children with disabilities and trained teachers to develop a program of movement techniques and coordination exercises for the students with disabilities.

In Latvia, grandparents who were farmers taught their grandson's class an important lesson about food, farming, and the cycle of nature. They invited the children in their grandson's class to a field trip to their farm. There, the children learned first-hand how grain grows, where vegetables come from, and also experienced seeing a newborn calf and baby chicks. From this outing, arranged by caring grandparents, the students in the class gained an appreciation of nature and a better understanding of the hard work involved with farm life.

In an Hispanic community in the United States, a group of grandparents who were native Spanish speakers volunteered their time to a school that had many Spanish-speaking children. They helped the children improve their English language skills because they were able to communicate with them in their native language. Grandparent-mentors teamed up with students to help with homework, and provide a sense of connection to their newly adopted country. Strong inter-generational bonds were formed, children improved their English language skills, and also gained an important link to caring people from their native country.

Grandparents are an important resource in all communities and often possess:

- Time (due to retirement)
- Interest (due to their connection with their grandchildren)
- A wealth of experience and valuable perspective
- Important skills from a lifetime of experience in many positions
- A strong desire to make meaningful contributions to societies

ARTISTS TAKE ACTION TO IMPROVE CHILDREN'S LIVES

In one neighborhood, a community had long been plagued by a lack of supervision for children after school. In fact, there are many places world-wide where children have few structured activities and lack proper adult supervision. In this case, one man, who had grown up in the neighborhood, took steps to make a difference. An artist and former boxer, he used his love of art as a starting point and organized an after-school group that gave children a place to be and provided them with important skills to use.

The former boxer's art studio was located on the streets where children frequently played. Used to seeing them hanging around with nothing to do, he developed a plan to put their energies to constructive work. He gathered a small group of students after school and invited them in to see his work. He provided them with art materials, paint, paintbrushes, and paper, and a place to be. He also used the time and opportunity to help resolve the children's neighborhood conflicts.

Each day after school a group of children assembled in his art studio to discuss problems they had encountered, and fights they had been in, either at home, at school, or in the neighborhood. He then suggested the children use a democratic method and vote on whose problem was the most significant that day. From that, they turned their life experiences into artistic expressions. The group then voted on which story "won" as the worst experience of the day, and that child's tale was chosen as the art subject of the day.

On one particular day, the "winning" story involved a child who had been physically beaten on the playground and whose playing cards had been stolen from him. The group received instruction and materials to turn the episode into a collage. Over several weeks and months, they were taught about color, proportion, paint technique, and were given the freedom and supplies to get to work. One of their collages was pictured in a local paper. The image was reproduced on notecards, T-shirts, and the group created other works to raise money, buy art supplies, and recruit more teachers to accommodate the growing number of children who wanted to join in this after-school "art" school.

There are many examples of how art has touched people's lives, and many ways that artists use their talents to benefit communities, from painting murals on run-down walls and billboards, to tiling parks, and even lending art-teachers-in-training to community associations for school credit. In all these cases, artists help their communities by:

- Providing constructive activities for children
- Teaching children to apply their abundant energies artistically and with purpose
- Teaching children to respect materials
- Teaching children fundamental concepts of teamwork and community as they often work together to produce murals and group projects

MOTHERS MAKE A DIFFERENCE: THE MILLION MOM MARCH

In the United States, more than 12 children are killed every day by guns. Gun violence is a severe public health hazard for children and adults alike. Between 1979 and 1997, 80,000 children and teenagers lost their lives to gun violence. Clearly, the statistics are grim. More painful are the individual stories of children's lives lost. The following is how dedicated mothers focused on this issue and organized the Million Mom March, a major march on Washington, D.C. which captured the attention of America, brought concerned parents into a politically active role (many for the first time), and placed significant pressure on the well-organized gun lobby in the United States.

The motivating force behind the organizing mothers' efforts was not personal experience with gun violence. Unlike so many mothers who had lost children to gun violence, the women who spearheaded the group had simply reached their own personal breaking points. They no longer wanted to be passive observers to daily news items about the effect of gun violence on children. The impetus for their actions came after a particularly violent incident at a day care center where a gunman had shot children that were the same ages as their own.

The saying "a picture is worth a thousand words" hit home in this case. Newspaper reports and photographs about the incident played a strong role in motivating the women. The media also played an important role in helping them carry their message around the country. A front-page photograph appeared in papers around America. It touched many heartstrings as it showed a human chain of children holding hands to get out of the path of the deranged shooter. Rather than simply cry over the photograph and the headlines, the women leaders took action and went to work to make a difference. They contacted the National Park Service in Washington, D.C. to apply for a permit for a march even though they had never done anything like this before. Initially, they estimated 10,000 marchers and 50 bus loads of people would attend. Nine months later, when the march took place, the movement had blossomed to the Million Mom March and estimates suggested hundreds of thousands of people attended the rally.

Their time frame for action was nine months, which they also pointed out was the same amount of time it takes for a child to be born. They also chose to hold the march on Mother's Day, which added to the publicity generated for the cause. Next, they developed clear and simple goals, from calling for mandatory trigger locks to gun registration. The group expertly used a series of public awareness strategies to help them convey their message. The short list of goals helped the group articu-late its purpose before the public, in newspaper coverage, local brochures, radio and television interviews. They also made use of a potent analogy that since car owners must register their cars, gun owners should have the same requirements.

As the date for the march approached, the airwaves were saturated with news about the group, its goals, as well as its opposition. While opposition on an issue can sometimes cause difficulties for action groups, in this case, opposition proved useful as it fueled the debate. This resulted in increased attention from the public. It generated strong reaction from the United States gun lobby, and the National Rifle Association (NRA). The use of mothers as the group's leaders and the target audience was a particularly effective element. Throughout history, mothers have often played prominent roles in objecting to war, protecting their children from human rights abuses and engaging in pickets, boycotts, and educational campaigns to promote their causes. The special role of motherhood and a useful linguistic advantage from the group's name helped promote the cause. In English, the name, Million Mom March, benefited from the alliteration, having three M's in the group's title which made the name easy to pronounce. Sometimes, an appealing name, a catchy phrase, or a well-designed logo can increase a group's visibility. In this case, a catchy name and an important cause helped attract an audience of listeners and participants.

To some organizers, the concept of the novice advocate or first-timer may seem like a liability. However, the energy newcomers brought to this action group was a strength. Many of those interviewed at the march confessed they didn't know that much about politics, or even gun control, and had never even been to a march before. However, like the organizers, the participants also "didn't like what they saw" and were no longer comfortable as bystanders in an increasingly violent society. Their decision not to accept the status quo was motivation for their involvement.

The final impact of the march, at this writing, is somewhat difficult to measure. However, already, it is clear that it was significant. The march was planned in the heat of presidential elections and had some effect on the positions of candidates toward gun control. One candidate for U.S. president proposed providing gun locks to those in his state. In Washington, D.C., where the march occurred, the pressure surrounding the march played a role in moving Washington, D.C. to accelerate a program in which the government "buys back" guns from its citizens.

Elsewhere around the country, free trigger locks were offered to citizens. The well-known American activist, Saul Alinsky once said, "If you aim for 100% and only get 30%, you're still ahead 30% from where you started." Even if the marchers fail to achieve all of their objectives, what is apparent is that in a short amount of time they made a significant impact. In brief, some of the factors that contributed were:

- A clear cause, with chilling facts that affected people's emotions
- Well-organized, committed leadership
- Excellent use of public awareness strategies and the media
- Taking a strong issue that has polarized the U.S.
- Using opposition to their advantage to engender debate and attention
- Clear-cut goals
- Energy of many first-time advocates

TEACHERS AND PARENTS MAKE A DIFFERENCE: A SCHOOL IN SLOVAKIA CHANGES ITS TRADITION

In a primary school in Slovakia, a traditional style of teaching had long been accepted. The teacher was in charge of the classroom and other adults were viewed as outsiders and unwelcome in school. Children were to be obedient receptors of rote learning that was based on textbook information. One teacher decided to try a new approach. As a result of her initiative and the support of willing parents, the classroom underwent a remarkable and positive change.

The teacher, in conjunction with willing parents, undertook a series of new teaching methods and also expanded the extent to which parents were allowed to be involved. Instead of a one-way street, the classroom became a two-way road, where parents and teachers joined together in activities during class and increased their communication after school. Cooperation between the school and the families was fostered when parents were treated as partners instead of outsiders.

One parent recounted how the teacher cultivated this new relationship with the parents as partners at a meeting where she asked, "If you are interested in something interesting or good at sports, visit our class and share your knowledge with us." No teacher had ever done this before. As a result of this simple request, many parents became involved in the school for the first time. Their involvement led to a number of positive experiences in the children's education and the community's cohesion. For instance:

• Parents organized get-togethers after school. These events helped families get to know their children's classmates better and understand what the children were doing in school. These informal gatherings were further enhanced through music and song, a favorite pastime of the community. They contributed to a more open sense of expression among students, parents, and teachers, which carried over into the classroom, where students also were better able to express themselves, in writing, speaking, and in art.

• For the first time, parents were actively encouraged to visit their children's classroom. Once seen as a place that parents did not belong, these classroom visits helped parents become better acquainted with their children's teacher, school, and classmates.

• One way the school reflected this change was by altering the traditional model of parent-teacher conferences. In the past, conferences were limited to a discussion of grades, and parents sat silently as the teacher presented them with their child's report card. In the new system, conversations about the child were encouraged and parents were able to discuss their child's behavior, personality, and interests with the classroom teacher.

• A special grandparents program was planned. One grandfather-gardener taught the class how to grow vegetables. Another grandfather-bricklayer helped the children make bricks and showed them how to build a house. Welcoming and including the older generation connected these caring grandparents to a wider community.

• Community service providers, such as firemen, doctors, and dentists, were invited to make special classroom visits and promote health and safety education. Previously remote figures in their children's lives, these professionals provided important opportunities for community members to become involved in local schools and bring needed information to children that could improve their health and well-being.

One boy in the class eloquently summed up the importance of the new and more open spirit where parents became partners in the school. From reading his touching letter, it is clear that the changes in his school improved his sense of community and made school like his "second family."

"I met my teacher in the first class. I was a very shy boy. She taught us four years. We did many activities, projects. We organized many field trips. Last year, our class, pupils, parents, and our teacher went to the seaside in Croatia. There it was very nice. The sea was beautiful. We visited two islands there. I was very happy when I swam with my teacher and we reached remote buoys in the sea.

Every evening our parents and teacher spoke, sang, and played cards. I think they knew each other much better. But days ran very quickly there and finally we had to leave the beautiful country and nice company. The rest of summer holiday I spent at home. In September, I was looking forward to meeting my friends and our teacher.

Every morning I knocked on the class door and I helped my teacher to prepare the classroom. Once she asked me, "Why do you knock when you go home?" It was true. My class was my second home. I thank my teacher for every-

thing she taught me. She will always have a place in my heart."

This situation illustrates how a willingness to change can have a significant impact.

- A community's willingness to try a new approach is critical to its success. New methods often meet some resistance. However, a willingness to try new things is vital when the benefits to children are at stake.

- It can improve parent-teacher cooperation and transform a classroom into a better environment to learn in and a better community to live in.

- Simple efforts, like after-school get-togethers, visits by other adults in the classroom, and field trips to local sites can play an important role in expanding children's understanding of their community. It can also improve children's and parents' experiences with their educational system and shape children as they grow and contribute to their communities.

TENDING GARDENS AND NURTURING COMMUNITIES

In many places around the world, neighborhoods have vacant lots that invite crime, lack sidewalks and clear spaces for children and adults to interact, and provide few "green" spaces as a refuge from the heat of city streets. Many communities have turned to neighborhood gardens to help address poor conditions and combat a host of problems, from crime to poor nutrition, to reducing food costs, to helping elderly gardeners tend their land. The following are stories collected from different corners of the world that revolve around the common theme of how community garden groups have rejuvenated neighborhoods.

- In one neighborhood, a high crime rate and lack of shade and relief from hot city streets had kept most children indoors. However, the community of "city farmers" partnered with local nurseries to donate plants, with seed companies to donate seeds, and used artists, teachers, and others to tend lots, build fences, and educate children about plant growth. During an experiment conducted by the children, they discovered that the temperature in their new green space was 11 degrees cooler, on average, than on the hot city streets.

- In Canada, a community garden helped an indigenous group of people find ways to celebrate their culture. They designed and developed a garden to honor traditional customs. Signs made by the community featured totems that were important to the native group. Certain areas of the garden faced south, a traditional way to connect with nature. The plants that were grown had ties to native plants and the community erected other structures, like a longhouse, reminiscent of their ancestor's designs and a symbol of pride.

- In one community, due to health problems, a group of elderly gardeners was no longer able to perform basic weeding of their garden plots. Many were concerned that their gardens were becoming overgrown. A local citizens' group paired senior citizen gardeners with eager novices who wanted to learn about planting. They held wheelbarrow races to attract attention and were able to match each person with a garden "teacher." The novices welcomed the training and the seasoned gardeners enjoyed the help and companionship.

- In one school, children used community gardens to supplement textbook learning about nature and science. The school curriculum was enhanced as children were able to observe first-hand the process of planting and growing. Children harvested and ate their own tomatoes, picked flowers for their parents, and made signs in art class to show the community that the garden was being cared for. Local religious groups sponsored sections of the garden and some of the produce grown was donated to families in need.

- Many communities suffer from a lack of places to gather or an increase of crime in run-down areas. Enhancing the appearance of communities can be a deterrent to crime. One group of urban gardeners reported that its gardeners often become the "eyes and ears" of the neighborhood and helped reduce neighborhood problems with their increased presence.

- A community's nutritional needs were also improved through community gardens. In one country, Chinese immigrants successfully grew bok choy. Elsewhere, poorer children were able to have healthier meals because they could harvest their own fruits and vegetables and save money on food at grocery stores. In many countries, immigrant groups have been able to grow their native plants, fruits, and vegetables and felt more at home in a foreign land.

The variety of experiences where community gardens have enhanced neighborhoods shows the important role that such efforts can play. Community gardens can help:

- Reduce crime when weeds and debris are cleared from vacant lots
- Offer spaces for recreation and relaxation to those who lack such areas
- Promote an interest and connection with nature
- Develop a sense of self-reliance as people grow their own food
- Improve nutrition and reduce costs when families are able to eat produce from local gardens
- Unite separate groups in the community as diverse groups join together to share a common interest

TEACHERS AND PARENTS FORM CULTURAL BRIDGES

There are many communities where children from a diversity of ethnic groups are new entrants into schools that have long been dominated by a majority culture. Although the names of the communities, the languages they speak, and the customs they practice vary, the issues are similar around the world. Should the children be allowed to speak their native language in school? How should teachers and schools deal with accommodating different customs, food preferences, ways of dress? While there are no standard answers to these complex questions, there are many cases where caring teachers, involved parents, eager students, and other thoughtful community members have worked together to benefit from the new diversity and improve educational opportunities for all. What follows is one case of how some of the problems a group of Latino children faced were addressed and how some of the needs in the classroom situation were met.

- The children, uncomfortable with speaking English, were reluctant to read English-language books out loud during reading time. Teachers expressed disappointment that their new students would not read and try to improve their language skills. They also were concerned that these children would fall behind their classmates in other academic areas. One of the parents approached the teachers to let them know that the children were embarrassed to read alone in front of the whole class and try their awkward new language. She proposed that a group of children read together so that no single child would feel singled out. This helped the children improve their language skills and ease their anxiety in class.

- Teachers also expressed concern that some of the newly arrived children were refusing to do individual classroom chores. The teacher had assumed that the students were being disruptive in their refusal. In fact, their reluctance was due to a cultural difference. Once the teacher was informed that the children were used to working as a community to do tasks at home and in their native land, she was able to use this model. She assigned two children at a time to classroom tasks, like cleaning chalkboards and tables. Carrying the tradition of community teamwork into the classroom improved the classroom experience for all.

- Another problem had been poor attendance at parent-teacher conferences. Although the teachers knew the parents cared, they were puzzled by the parents' absence at important meetings. One parent who had lived in the area much longer than others and spoke both languages was also able act as a bridge between the two communities. She contacted the teacher and let her know that the parents, uncomfortable with their own English language skills were reluctant to come to school functions. She also recalled her own experience as a child, where she had been forced to write, "I will not speak Spanish in school," which still made her uncomfortable in a school environment. Because she was motivated to bridge the cultural gap, she agreed to act as translator at parent-teacher conferences. In time, as the children's language skills improved, they were able to act as translators for their parents. Conferences became more productive and the new dialogue between the parents and teachers shed light on issues and allowed both sides to construct solutions to address problematic situations.

This story shows the number of important issues that can confront a community, a school, children, parents, and teachers as they cope with change. Working together can alleviate many of the potential problems. Cooperation resulted in:

- Improved communication between parents and teachers benefited the children. The teachers found that once the students were allowed to work in pairs, they became more eager participants in classroom discussions, better helpers and more confident readers. Their academic skills flourished when they no longer felt singled out.

- The improved experiences the children had in school contributed to making the parents feel more welcome in their children's schools and therefore, also in their new communities.

- With the help of translators, participation at parent-teacher conferences rose dramatically. Improving dialogue in a community enabled the two groups to work well together to tackle ongoing issues as they appeared.

CONCLUSION

Parents are always encouraging their children to learn new skills. From the time they are infants, and throughout their lives, parents are their children's teachers. Sometimes, they teach by example, and show them how to tie their shoes, hold a spoon, or use a pencil. As children grow, the lessons and methods parents use to teach also change. Children learn new things from many sources beyond the world of their parents, from their teachers, to their peers, to the broader community.

Adults too are always learning. This manual is intended to play a part in helping adults who are interested in learning how to make a difference in their communities. By showing how others have accomplished change, by demonstrating some of the steps it takes to make a difference, and by encouraging readers to give advocacy methods a try, it is hoped that parents and others who want to intervene, will now know how to be effective and make a difference.

The information in this book is designed to help people committed to improving their communities. However, the real test will come from putting these newfound skills into practice. Admittedly, learning new skills and trying new approaches can be both exciting and challenging. First steps are sometimes awkward, but, ultimately, with practice they grow into steady strides. Rather than remaining concerned spectators, readers can become active participants in improving their lives and those of other families in the communities in which they live.

REFERENCES AND INTERNET RESOURCES

References

Boal, J.T. (July 1999). *Be a Global Force of One in Your Hometown.* Publisher: John T. Boal.

Bobo, K. et al. (1996). *Organizing for Social Change: A Manual for Activists in the 1990s.* Santa Ana, CA: Seven Locks Press.

Dombro, A.L. et al. (1996). *Community Mobilization: Strategies to Support Young Children and Their Families.* New York: Families and Work Institute.

Gentili et al. (1993). *How to Organize an Effective Parent/Advocacy Group and Move Bureaucracies.* Chicago: Family Resource Center on Disabilities.

Kingsley, G.T. et al. (April 1997). *Community Building: Coming of Age.* Baltimore, MD: The Development Training Institute.

Kretzmann, J. P. and J.L. McKnight. (1993). *Building Communities from the Inside Out: A Path Toward Finding and Mobilizing a Community's Assets.* Chicago: ACTA Publications.

Mattessich, P. et al. (1997). *Community Building: What Makes It Work: A Review of Factors Influencing Successful Community Building.* Saint Paul, MN: Amherst H. Wilder Foundation.

New, Anne L. (1991). *Raise More Money for Your Nonprofit Organization.* New York: The Foundation Center.

Schorr, Lisbeth. (1998). *Common Purpose: Strengthening Families and Neighborhoods to Rebuild America.* New York, NY: Doubleday.

STAR Project of Delphi International. *Public Policy Advocacy: Women for Social Change in the Yugoslav Successor States.* Washington, DC: STAR Project.

Internet Resources

Connect for Kids. www.connectforkids.org. (A web page for parents and community advocates, funded by the Benton Foundation, Washington, DC.)

National Community Building Network. www.ncbn.org (An alliance of individuals and organizations that is based in Oakland, CA and works to reduce poverty and create social and economic opportunity through comprehensive community building strategies.)

Points of Light Foundation. www.pointsoflight.org (A foundation based in Washington, DC that is devoted to promoting volunteerism